Appearance & Reality

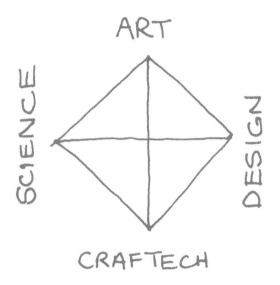

ART

SCIENCE

DESIGN

CRAFTECH

Contents

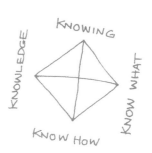

Preface **xii**

The Quadriform Models; Specialists and Generalists; Text; Images; Appearance is Deceiving.

Introduction **2**

Disciplines; Comprehension; Language; Sensory Experience; Sensory Seeing; Light and Color; Problems of Seeing; Critical Seeing; Dichotomies and Quadriforms.

CHAPTER 1. The visual contrasts and elements **24**

Visual Contrasts; Visual Elements; Point; Line; Shape; Form; Value and Color.

CHAPTER 2. Composition **40**

Composition in 2 Dimensions; Depth; Forces and Tension; Perspective; Proportion and Scale. Composition in 3 Dimensions; Problem of Illusion; Modeling with Computers; Discrete Objects; Objects and Relations; Enclosures.

CHAPTER 3. Expression **60**

Emotion and Expression; Light; Color; Marks; Line; Shape and Value; Color; Surfaces and Solids; Structures and Enclosures; How the "isms" Fit.

CHAPTER 4. Pattern **74**

History and Culture; Imagery and Motif; Iconic Images; Organization of Motif; Implied Movement; Dazzle in Pattern; Actual Movement; Media and Method; Patterns from Nature; Fractals.

CHAPTER 5. Transformation **86**

Multiple Intelligence; Preconscious Creativity; Physical Creativity; Problem Solving; Scientific Method; Paying Attention.

CHAPTER 6. Self and Other **100**

Diversity; Self; Subject; Object; Context.

CHAPTER 7. Communication **112**

Communication; Modes of Communication; Image Making; Accurate Observation; Formalism and Beauty; Lyrical and Fantastic; Analytic Observer; Descriptive Devices.

CHAPTER 8. Community **126**

Fit and Loose Fit; Location and Subject; Location and Identity; Representation; Community Ecology; Place, Space and Time; Nurturing Culture; Rights and Responsibilities.

CHAPTER 9. Region **138**

Between Macro and Micro Views; City as Region; Origin and Original; Stories and Images; Organization; Material and Method.

CHAPTER 10. Critical Methods **150**

Critical Performance; Communications Method; Relationship of Evaluator to Maker; Intention of the Maker; Precedents and Context; Critical Disciplines; Journalistic Description; Scholarly Analysis; Pedagogical Discussion; Popular Opinion; Critical Means; What Does It Express? What Is It Telling Us? How Is It Used? What Does It Look Like? Critical Process.

Bibliography **171**

Index **174**

Published by Cambium Press

PO Box 909

Bethel, CT 06801 USA

Tel 203-778-2782   Fax 203-778-2785

Cambium Press is a division of Cambium Associates, Inc.

ISBN 1-892836-05-x

First printing: April 2000

Printed in Hong Kong

Library of Congress Cataloging-in-Publication Data

Hogbin, Stephen

    Appearance & Reality: a visual handbook for artists, designers, and makers : Australia, Canada, Great Britain, United States of America / Stephen Hogbin.

       p. cm

   Includes bibliographical references and index

   ISBN 1-892836-05-X

    1. Visual communication in art. 2. Visual perception. 3. Creation (Literary, artistic, etc.) I. Title: Appearance and reality. II. Title.

N7430.5 .H64 2000

701—dc21   99-088964

To the inspired teachers

George Bryant
Adrian Duckworth
David Pye
Don McKinley

Contents

List of Images   **viii**

The Models   **ix**

Preface   **xii**

The Quadriform Models; Specialists and Generalists; Text; Images;
Appearance is Deceiving. Acknowledgements.

Introduction   **2**

Disciplines; Comprehension; Language; Sensory Experience; Sensory Seeing; Light
and Color; Problems of Seeing; Critical Seeing; Dichotomies and Quadriforms.

CHAPTER 1. The Visual Contrasts and Elements   **24**

Visual Contrasts; Visual Elements; Point; Line; Shape; Form; Value and Color.

CHAPTER 2. Composition   **40**

Composition in 2 Dimensions; Depth; Forces and Tension; Perspective; Proportion
and Scale. Composition in 3 Dimensions; Problem of Illusion; Modeling with
Computers; Discrete Objects; Objects and Relations; Enclosures.

CHAPTER 3. Expression   **60**

Emotion and Expression; Light; Color; Marks; Line; Shape and Value; Color;
Surfaces and Solids; Structures and Enclosures; How the "isms" Fit.

CHAPTER 4. Pattern   **74**

History and Culture; Imagery and Motif; Iconic Images; Organization of Motif;
Implied Movement; Dazzle in Pattern; Actual Movement; Media and Method;
Patterns from Nature; Fractals.

CHAPTER 5. Transformation   **86**

Multiple Intelligence; Preconscious Creativity; Physical Creativity; Problem Solving; Scientific Method; Paying Attention.

CHAPTER 6. Self and Other   100

Diversity; Self; Subject; Object; Context.

CHAPTER 7. Communication   112

Communication; Modes of Communication; Image Making; Accurate Observation; Formalism and Beauty; Lyrical and Fantastic; Analytic Observer; Descriptive Devices.

CHAPTER 8. Community   126

Fit and Loose Fit; Location and Subject; Location and Identity; Representation; Community Ecology; Place, Space and Time; Nurturing Culture; Rights and Responsibilities.

CHAPTER 9. Region   138

Between Macro and Micro Views; City as Region; Origin and Original; Stories and Images; Organization; Material and Method.

CHAPTER 10. Critical Methods   150

Critical Performance; Communications Method; Relationship of Evaluator to Maker; Intention of the Maker; Precedents and Context; Critical Disciplines; Journalistic Description; Scholarly Analysis; Pedagogical Discussion; Popular Opinion; Critical Means; What Does It Express? What Is It Telling Us? How Is It Used? What Does It Look Like? Critical Process.

Bibliography   171

Index   174

List of Images, Makers, and Regions

2 To Forgotten Fleets, *Read & Conway*
SOUTHEAST ENGLAND

8 Gardenscape Series #17, *Kris Rosar*
CENTRAL CANADA

12 Porcelain Bowl, *Victor Greenaway*
SOUTHEAST AUSTRALIA

18 Thermonuclear Parabola Cooker, *David Baty & Kevin Brewer*
NORTHERN CALIFORNIA

24 Grandmother, *Kathy Bunnell*
NORTHERN CALIFORNIA

28 Bruce Peninsula Health Services, *Dunlop Farrow*
CENTRAL CANADA

32 Untitled Red and Green, *Emma Sullivan*
SOUTHEAST ENGLAND

38 Light Timber Construction, *Anthony Lake*
SOUTHEAST AUSTRALIA

40 Subsurface Dragonfly, *Joan Hawksbridge*
CENTRAL CANADA

42 B+, *Les Bicknell*
SOUTHEAST ENGLAND

46 Scorched Ash Pots, *Stephen Broadley*
SOUTHEAST ENGLAND

48 Sterling Silver Coffee Pot, *Hendrick Forster*
SOUTHEAST AUSTRALIA

50 Bowl, *John Woollard*
SOUTHEAST ENGLAND

54 Sculpture Moving Slowly in a Thousand Intricate Pieces, *Sha-Sha Higby*
NORTHERN CALIFORNIA

60 Caryatid 1, *Eva Volny*
SOUTHEAST AUSTRALIA

64 Untitled 1995, *Kenneth Feldsott*
NORTHERN CALIFORNIA

68 House on Wheels, *Mark Dixon*
SOUTHEAST ENGLAND

70 Bethesda Cemetery, *Michelle Carleton-McGillis*, CENTRAL CANADA

72 Gothic Novel, *Marilyn Campbell*
CENTRAL CANADA

74 Night Sky, *Clive Murry-White*
SOUTHEAST AUSTRALIA

78 Orfordness, *Glynn Thomas*
SOUTHEAST ENGLAND

82 Plate, *Rick Yoshimoto*
NORTHERN CALIFORNIA

84 Green Fish, *Jim Hong Louie*
CENTRAL CANADA

86 Rite of Passage, *Anne Greenwood*
SOUTHEAST AUSTRALIA

90 New Grange Bowl 2, *Mary Crehan*
SOUTHEAST ENGLAND

94 Superbowl Energy Free Waterer, *SPI*
CENTRAL CANADA

98 Grace: Homage to Earth and Sky for Food and Water, *Kathleen Edwards*
NORTHERN CALIFORNIA

100 Silent Boats, *Allen Smutylo*
CENTRAL CANADA

104 Miss Sailing Arrives for Sunday School, *Leanne Edwards*
SOUTHEAST AUSTRALIA

105 Laird's Landing Letters: Water Conservation, *Clayton Lewis*
NORTHERN CALIFORNIA

108 Mage, *JB Blunk*
NORTHERN CALIFORNIA

110 Craftsmanship, *Frances Evelegh*
SOUTHEAST ENGLAND

112 Opened by Censor, *Kit Artig*
NORTHERN CALIFORNIA

114 Township, *William Young*
SOUTHEAST AUSTRALIA

120 The Move, *Sue Brinkhurst*
SOUTHEAST ENGLAND

122 Dorothy C, *Blake Debosegai*
CENTRAL CANADA

126 Magdalene Bridge, *Liz Moon*
SOUTHEAST ENGLAND

130 Confessional, *Pat Waters*
SOUTHEAST AUSTRALIA

132 Burning Labyrinth, *Miz-Maze Theater*
NORTHERN CALIFORNIA

136 Fifth Season Cycle Center, *Clough Goss Hogbin Louie Osthoff*
CENTRAL CANADA

138 Canadology: Rite of Winter Solstice, *John Boyle*
CENTRAL CANADA

142 Elmsead Market, *Jason Gathorn-Hardy*
SOUTHEAST ENGLAND

144 Bog Heap with Two Alders, *Sue Englebry*
NORTHERN CALIFORNIA

146 Grape Basket for Growers, *Pat Dale*
SOUTHEAST AUSTRALIA

152 Stoneware Vase, *Steve Irvine*
CENTRAL CANADA

156 N. Gravity 2, *Anthea Williams*
SOUTHEAST AUSTRALIA

160 Garden building at Woodbridge Lodge, *Hugh Pilkington*,
SOUTHEAST ENGLAND

164 Man Ray's Kiss, *Charles Hobson*
NORTHERN CALIFORNIA

The Models

PREFACE

INTRODUCTION

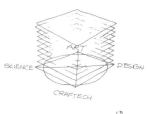

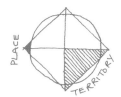

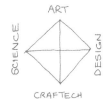

CHAPTER 1. The visual contrasts and elements

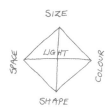

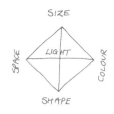

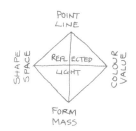

CHAPTER 2. Composition

CHAPTER 3. Expression

CHAPTER 5. Transformation

CHAPTER 6. Self and Other   **CHAPTER 7.** Communication

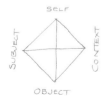    

CHAPTER 8. Community

CHAPTER 9. Region

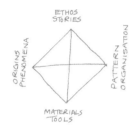

CHAPTER 10. Critical Methods

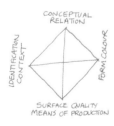

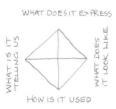

Preface

Working in the various visual arts and different disciplines for more than 30 years has made me aware of their similarities and differences. Each one has its own codes and aspirations. Often there is overlap, especially when working on a large project, such as a building, that requires a team of specialists. This book looks at the fundamentals of the visual world to see where there is overlap and possibly consensus. *Appearance and Reality* is a synthesis, not an in-depth focus on the particular detail of any discipline.

Throughout this investigation of *Appearance and Reality*, the environment has been of great concern. If the production and realization of a creative idea damages a healthy environment, there is absolutely no point in pursuing the activity.

THE MODELS

The models—quadriforms—used throughout the book illustrate some fundamental relationships between perception and the various disciplines. They will help the beginner as well as the professional to asses thoughts, feelings, responses, and actions towards the project. Each quadriform shows four relationships that continue to build through the book. The quadriform is a device for avoiding dualism and the confrontation implicit in the simplistic binary choice of one over the other. Nothing is so simple that it can be placed only or always in four ways, but this does offer a start to the inquiry, and a useful checklist for working on projects. Sometimes the four choices offer a fit, though sometimes it is a loose

fit and others times it is a misfit. Since the misfits are at a minimum and the quadriform pattern is strikingly repetitive, we can expect it to be a pertinent place to start. It is important to think of the egalitarian nature of the quadriform. All four aspects are equally important, indeed the visual fabric may unravel if one thread is left out. The elegant simplicity of a neat experiment carries with it the danger of losing important phenomena, so it is well to think of the quadriforms as a broad map and not as a substitute for the complexity of life.

Although specialists and generalists represent two poles, *Appearance and Reality* places them in the same context. I believe that everybody leans into and out of being a specialist or a generalist during a given project and as life progresses. Life is richer for the two extremes of specialized and generalized experience, while most people live and work between the poles on a spectrum of colorfully interrelated possibilities. I tend to lean toward the generalist. To write this book I had to read the specialist texts and place them in an order, simplifying and positioning, in the context of *Appearance and Reality*. I am indebted to those original sources and recognize those most important to me in the bibliography.

The text comes from many years of working and thinking about the essentials of living and working as a visual artist in a particular region. It was written over many years, and I know it is difficult to sit down and read straight through. For me

It is the flag that moves? Is it the wind? Neither, said Hui-Neng, the sixth Chian Buddhist Patriarch of China: It is your mind.

☙

> The true mystery of the world
> is the visible, not the invisible.
>
> *OSCAR WILDE*

insight has always come a little at a time, when the time was right for me to see. Some ideas took years to penetrate my perception. Appearance and Reality should be read as needed.

THE IMAGES

The images have been selected by four people from three continents, four nations, and four regions. The images present many different communities and individuals. The intention is to elaborate the possibilities, not to present a centrist, definitive, or exclusive profile of any group. The problems of inclusion are unending and will always be that way in a social ecology. The images reflect the qualities of their region and context, and I hope that readers will, by seeing how others have created themselves, discover their own regional character through their own work.

That regions have particular characteristics and concerns, and that these can be seen in the works of art, craft, and design made there, is central to the concept of this book. The region and the communities within it constitutes the broad context in which artists, designers, and makers live, among myriad other people who may view their works and respond to them.

The regions were chosen simply because I had visited, taught, or lived in them, I had personal experience with their characteristics, similarities and differences, and I knew people living there who could help me select the images and prepare commentaries on them. By intent, none of the four chosen centers on a large city. It is important to demonstrate that the imaginative experience is as active in the country as it is in the city, and that the process of creation is the same in either place, even though the problems of

materials, politics, and subject matter may be different. Indeed, many artists, designers and makers themselves move easily from the metropolis to small towns and regional centers, refashioning their own context and experience as they become more embedded in one place or the other.

APPEARANCE

Appearance is deceiving, says the aphorism. The title *Appearance and Reality* joints to the problem of appearances. There is more than one way to see any appearance. It is always necessary to think critically while enjoying the miraculous phenomena of the visual world, of how we see, and of why we create our own unique places to be.

There is always more than meets the eye. When people create they start with a personal truth, and end with an illusion about the appearance of reality. The reality is that nature carries on becoming, growing, eroding, and reforming. We all fit within this continuum. Each person's true reality may be unconscious and not something that can be assigned with a label or simple meaning. The foundation of human nature is instinct but through the intellect we attempt to formulate our experiences so that we can communicate with one another. *Appearance and Reality* is based in knowledge, but I am keenly aware of the need for intuition and spontaneity to be part of the creative process. The reality of appearance is extremely personal but on occasion we can ironically agree on what is our reality.

Acknowledgments

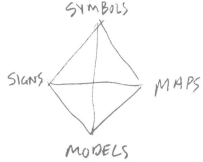

In 1969, as part of a design course I was teaching, I started to investigate simple maps of experience. Other instructors exchanged ideas with me on this search for a framework to aid the students in comprehending the visual experience. Joyce Chown, Sheila Lamb, and particularly Don McKinley of Sheridan College, were endlessly tolerant and interested in my proposals. These maps became somewhat involved and complex. The quadriform evolved in 1975/6 as I wrote my first book, *Woodturning: The Purpose of the Object.*

Vic Wood and Norman Creighton of Melbourne State College became my sounding board in the next round of investigation. Carol Hanks pointed out the progression of language over time and its influence on perception. Since then I have pulled out these maps for various lectures, seminars, and courses, and continued to find them a source of interest in thinking about the whole. In 1992 Allen Smutylo suggested I teach the design course again. Out came all my notes and once again I engaged with ideas about the visual experience, but this time I resolved to place the ideas sequentially for a book. Inevitably my students have taught me a great deal because without an audience much of the information could not have been clarified into simple sentences.

Throughout my writing career

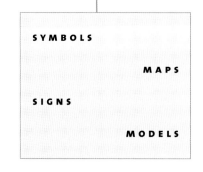

Maryann Hogbin has challenged my ideas and helped my comprehension of language. John Kelsey, publisher and editor-in-chief at Cambium Press, has been editing my periodic essays since the mid 1970s, showing me how to construct ideas so others might understand. The idea for image selection came from John Boyle. He had proposed an exhibition of work from countries in the shade of powerful nations. This suggested the possibility of working from a regional rather than a national context. The slogan "Think globally, act locally" suggested the means to see how others experience their sense of place and their culturally shared experiences.

Norman Creighton (southeastern Australia), Sarah Evelegh (southeastern England), and Janice Sandeen (northern California) acted as researchers and picture editors for their regions (I selected the images for my own region, south-central Canada). Prof. Creighton recently retired from Monash University in Australia. He has a background in working with metals and is a keen observer of the regional experience. Sarah

Evelegh of Sussex, England, is a practicing architectural interior designer with a broad appreciation for art, craft, and design. Janice Sandeen lives in Bolinas, CA, has a background in sculpture and furniture making, and has a keen sense of the need to care for the natural and built environment. Without them, *Appearance and Reality* would not have spoken to our collective understanding of the regional experience.

The process of selecting the images took more than a year to complete. The selectors read an early draft of the manuscript, then visited with the artists to choose groups of images. I evaluated how well they would work within *Appearance and Reality* and wrote the commentaries. The selectors then reviewed my comments with the artists.

Throughout this long process the artists were generous with their time and thoughtful advice. Without the artistsí works, their enthusiasms and insights, the project could not have happened.

Thank you to the readers, Ken Dour and particularly Simon Carrier, who looked at the final text and gave their critical evaluation, helping to refine the material into the book you hold in your hand. Finally, the lively appearance of the book itself is the design work of Jeanne Criscola and Peggy Bloomer, and I am grateful for their insightful contribution.

Stephen Hogbin
Owen Sound, ON, Canada
September, 1999

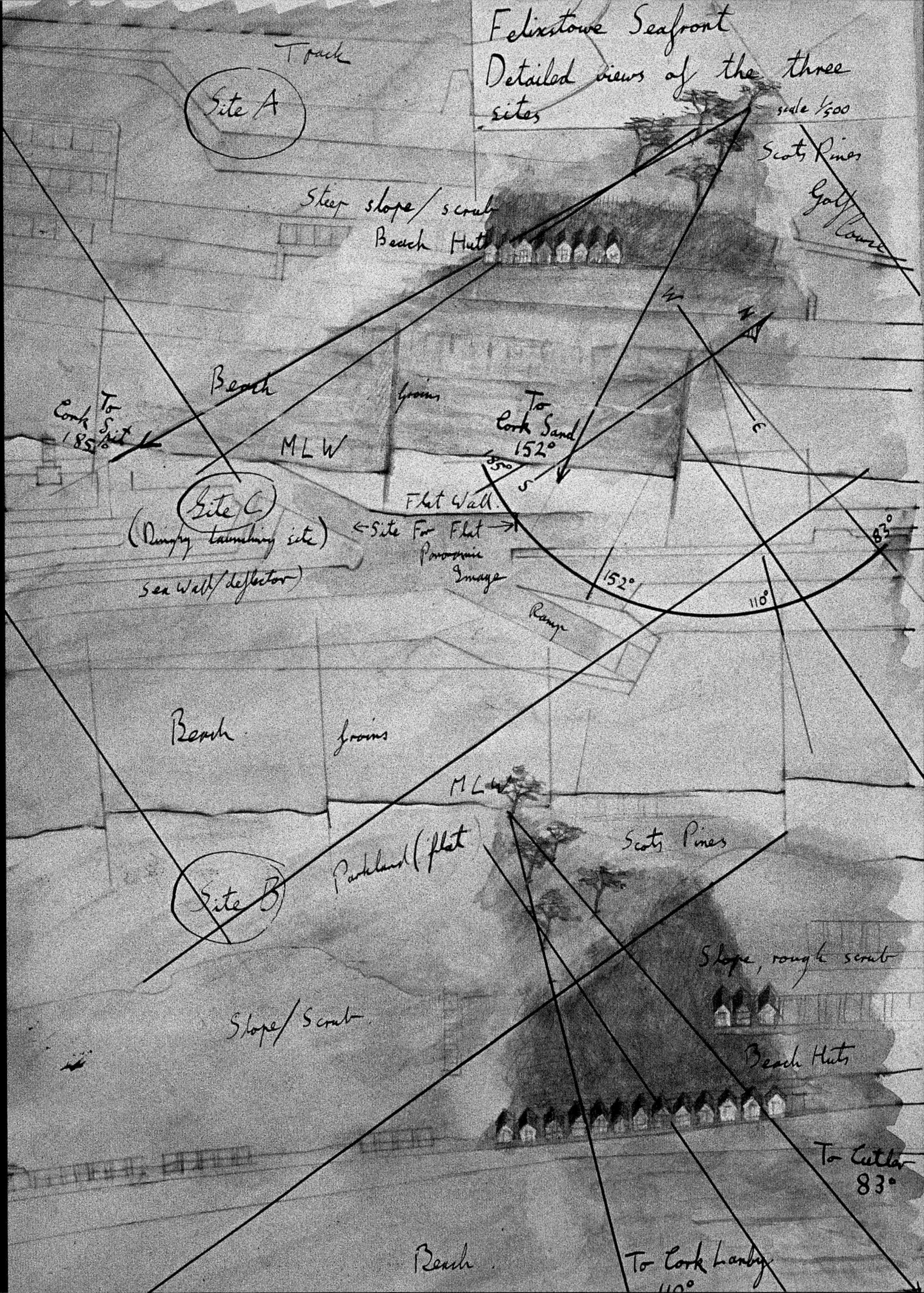

Felixstowe Seafront
Detailed views of the three sites
scale 1/500

Site A

Track

Scots Pines

Golf Course

Steer slope/scrub
Beach Huts

Beach

To S pit 185°
Cork

MLW

To Cork Sand 152°

Site C
(Dinghy launching site)

Sea Wall (deflector)

Flat Wall

← Site For Flat →
Panoramic Image

Range

152°

110°

83°

Beach   groins

MLW

Parkland (flat

Scots Pines

Site B

Slope, rough scrub

Slope / Scrub.

Beach Huts

To Cutler 83°

Beach.

To Cork Lanby
110°

To Forgotten Fleets
1995

Concept Drawing
Simon Read and Ros Conway
Woodbridge, Suffolk, UK

To Forgotten Fleets is an installation less concerned with sensory appreciation than with a conceptual relationship. With the knowledge that sailing vessels used the parallax relationship of landmarks ashore to help avoid the North Sea shoals—and that these could be anything from deliberately sited towers, beacons, or lines of trees to happy coincidences of prominent buildings and landscape features—Read and Conway proposed to established their own co-ordinates by planting trees upon alignments with approaches to the port of Harwich and Felixstowe and the River Deben. Read and Conway explain, *"A little over nine miles North by East of here is an avenue of trees known as the Butley Clumps; these were planted in 1794 by the Marquis of Donegal and are organized as groups of four beech trees each with a single pine at the center. Their surfaces are scarred with generations of carving which, with some patience and a lot of looking, may be discerned as ships and boats consistent with what would have been familiar around this coast in the late 19th century. Identifiable to the extent that the bark has stretched over the years, and inevitably to perish with the trees, these little drawings bear witness to a time when the North Sea was busy with huge trading and fishing fleets. This work... is dedicated to those fleets. The Scots pines have been planted to align with the courses taken habitually by vessels through the shoals... For each tree there is a companion photographic image, taken from the drawings of the boats upon the bark of the beech trees of the Butley Clumps."*

The other part of this installation is at the Dip Felixstowe, where the presence of vessels sandblasted into relief in a concrete wall evoke "the elusive subtlety of a memory" to Forgotten Fleets.

Introduction

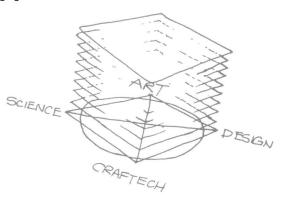

The title **APPEARANCE** suggests that we are concerned not only with the way we see the world, but also with the way the world emerges in us and how we make appearances respond to it. "Appearance" is an analysis of what is and also what things may become. In many ways "appearance" needs to be revelatory, or else we see, but do not experience or comprehend what is around us. I am interested in insight, organization, making, communication, and also in how these fuse in the experience of "appearance."

> Experience is a complex net of events connecting different junctions which align, alternate, overlap, and combine. Rather than defining or determining the junctions... generate the space, color, texture, and rhythm of the whole.
>
>

Objects have an appearance and the first four chapters of the book consider how their visual qualities are structured and constructed. Often the object appears outside us, and even detached from us. The second half of the book recognizes that all we see is happening in the mind. Our response to appearance occurs in an instant, influenced not only by the experience of the moment but also by our past experience. The appearance of any object takes on significance because we react to it, think about it, and imagine what it is again. We construct appearance from early childhood and continue to reform it throughout life. Early realities still

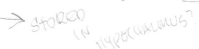

DISCIPLINES

COMPREHENSION

SENSORY SEEING

CRITICAL SEEING

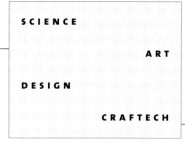

SCIENCE

ART

DESIGN

CRAFTECH

influence present experience. In times of stress, images and objects offer a constant. The child is drawn to the experience of a blanket or toy because it is constant. Adults also, although perhaps not so willfully, use the appearance of things as a point of constancy. Appearance in memory is as important as appearance in reality—memory operates as a stabilizing influence on experience.

Four approaches to appearance will be considered. These are the disciplines of **ART**, **DESIGN**, **CRAFT/TECHNOLOGY**, and **SCIENCE**. In each discipline there are, more often than not, overlapping concerns. The great separations of approach, whether imagined or actual, often result from control exerted by the discipline: the focus is necessary to make something work. Which model best describes the relationship of one discipline to another? Perhaps it is a continuum of merging concerns, rather than a series of discrete intellectual and physical boxes. Initially the division by discipline helps to break things down, in order to build them up into a comprehensive whole.

The following example suggests how one discipline may focus specifically on quite different concepts. Painters develop a sensitivity to color so acute they will see a greater range of color than most people can detect. Paul Klee said, "Color possesses me. I no longer have to pursue it. It will possess me always. I know it...color and I are one. I am a painter." The craftsperson's sense of touch and sight, and the ability to fit and work a material with quick deft movements, is unmatched. The architect's ability is to create space in which human activities can take place. The Museum of Civilization in Ottawa, Canada is exceptional for its spatial arrangement on the site and its organization of activities within the complex, computer-generated form. Scientists are practiced at observation. The smallest variation in an experiment is registered. Firestone melted rubber on the hot plate and noticed that the spoiled, hardened rubber was ideal for making tires. But what is significant is that the architect is interested in color and the painter observes acutely, the scientist appreciates an elegant form, and the craftsperson comprehends spatial arrangements in order to fit things together. While some specialization may be necessary, it is imperative that people in each discipline have a working ability in each of the other fields of concerns.

The models, or quadriforms are a playful way to see relationships. Like kites, they can be flown to test ideas in the winds of change.

DISCIPLINES

Although the simplified model or kite of Art, Craft/Technology, Design and Science indicates separations that are definitive, I see them as analogous to a baseball game where the home plate is where the person starts and the three other disciplines are represented by the bases. In any project it will be necessary to touch base with each of the disciplines. Sometimes it may be necessary to stay at one base for extended periods; other times a home run will take the player quickly around the field. In the kites used throughout the text you will see that sometimes the base is the focus and at other times the focus is the space between the bases. As the players reach each base they pass through a territory of the adjoining discipline. At the home plate of the kite I am at craft/technology. I run to the first base through the territory of craft and design, I travel through the territory to get to the next base. The starting point or home plate may change to any one of the disciplines—art, design, craft/technology, or science. The analogy is useful but need not be taken further. The kites throughout the book will present the discipline as sometimes a place and sometimes a territory. There can be a strong affinity between certain quadrants, such as art and science, or design and technology. The point is that, regardless of labels we choose or have attached to us, it is necessary to pass through various disciplines to experience, create and comprehend the whole.

Changing workplaces may be like changing cultures—an invigorating, humbling, mind-expanding experience. Relocating the technologist to an artist's studio, the artist to a laboratory, the scientist to a woodworking shop, or the craftsperson to a design office, may well expand the scope and propel the individual into unexpected new relationships. Conversely, there may be more to learn in a lifetime in any one of the disciplines, so why press for the crossover? How can one possibly do it all? The primary reason is that cultural displacement develops empathy for other disciplines and other people. It is important to not try and do it all at once. Do one thing and keep doing one thing until you do it well, then regroup and move on.

COMPREHENSION

Understanding develops through **KNOWING** (the subject), **KNOW-HOW** (to do something), **KNOW-WHAT** (to do) and (increasing) **KNOWLEDGE**. This is

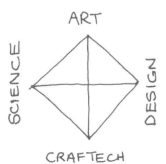

ART

SCIENCE

DESIGN

CRAFTECH

> Pictures become a kind of writing as soon as they are meaningful: like writing, they call for a lexis…. We shall therefore take language, discourse, speech etc. to mean any significant unit of synthesis, whether verbal or visual: a photograph will be a kind of speech for us in the same way as a newspaper article…
>
> ❧
> ROLAND BARTHES

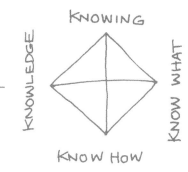

the art of knowing, design and know-what to do, the craft/technology of know-how, and science of increasing knowledge. Although neither a theory, a principle, nor a law, this is a simplified way to think about different approaches to the visual experience. It may well be based in the system of memory: the mind remembers different kinds of things in different ways. This is not a fact but an hypothesis which, by the end of the book, may seem convincing.

Separating the ways of seeing is egalitarian in approach, not favoring one discipline, but rather comprehending the importance and place of each activity within a vital, connected, and integrated society. There are moments when "knowing" must be given up to the risk of "not knowing." By defining the world we draw lines around it and objectify the experience as knowledge. To gain deeper insights it is necessary to let go of knowledge and allow the experiences of life to merge and dissolve into experience. We can always think about an experience later.

MEMORY is the store from which we reflect on experiences. There are different ways of remembering. A deep sense of connection to the whole, a complex procedure, an emotional response to a situation, and a series of facts will each be recalled from different parts of the mind. These

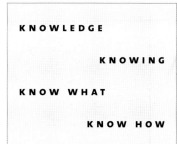

may represent the **FOUR SYSTEMS OF MEMORY**. The mind remembers in different ways for different things. People have different mental or memory strengths that influences their personal direction. Some people are fascinated by images, others engrossed in subjects, and others are captivated by how things are constructed. Two-dimensional and three-dimensional projects may share similarities, although the skills for each may be distinct, different ways of knowing the world. The **INVENTOR'S** project is usually different from the **PRODUCTION MANAGER'S**. The **RESTORER** or **FIXER** of things is different from the **MAKER** who conceives the project in relationship to the whole. The inventor restorer, maker and production manager may well be different people who at times will have tried each way of being in the world. Perhaps the one element that connects across these different experiences is the study of language and semiotics.

The language of the visual arts is influenced by the written word. To amplify diagrams, drawings, and illustrations, words are used. This may not always be the case. Some images are better off without words. An image is at its strongest when it needs no words, but resonates with the viewer. As the saying goes, "a picture is worth a thousand words;" about one thousand typed words could be replaced by an 8-1/2" x 11" or an A4 sized picture; usually you can have one or the other, there is seldom room for both. In the digital domain, pictorial information will take more space. A picture might require one megabyte (some eight million digital bits) of storage, depending on its size and the fineness of the detail recorded, whereas one thousand words of text might require as little as eight kilobytes (some sixty four thousand digital bits) of storage. However, whatever the space limitations, talking about a work adds clarity, passive looking gives way to active analysis, and a perceptive seeing becomes a conceptual understanding. There is a symbiosis between word and image, where the one will support the other to mutually advance comprehension. It is also clear that some works are more rewarding when they are explained. We accept that science needs to be explained to the observer—some of it I shall probably never fully understand. Some art will also have to be explained because it goes beyond a sensual appreciation of form to include, for example, a linguistic underpinning, a narrative, an iconic and a more difficult ironic meaning.

Central to our understanding of the disciplines in the visual arts is our comprehension of the meanings that are carried by the words ART, CRAFT/TECHNOLOGY, DESIGN, and SCIENCE. These words have been redefined through centuries of evolution as the processes used to comprehend the world through work and, in particular, the activity of the imagination, have adapted to new circumstances.

> The language we use to reflect ourselves. whether that language is the visual, literary or performing arts, the expression of culture is about placing the self in the universe. that placing of ourselves in the universe, defining ourselves in the universe, is a spiritual act. an act of transformation; of transcendence.
>
> ❧
> **MONIQUE MOJICA**
> KUNA AND RAPPAHANNOCK FIRST NATIONS,
> TORONTO-BASED ACTOR AND PLAYWRIGHT

LANGUAGE

What is the difference between a STUDIO, a WORKSHOP, an OFFICE, and a LABORATORY? Each term is loaded with histories, connotations, and expectations. The root of the word "art" starts with "ars" and then it comes through time as ARS, ARSARTIUM, ARTIFICIUM, ARTIFICE, TECHNE, TECHNIC, and TECHNOLOGY. As the word evolves it picks up or develops the four disciplines. ARS is Latin for skill in joining something, combining and working it. "Ars" is also an abbreviated form for arsenal but on this occasion I shall leave that as an explosive aside.

ARSARTIUM is Latin for the art of arts that is logic, thus the skill in joining something, combining and working it gains an intellectual and imaginative connotation rather than a physical character.

ARTIFICIUM is the display of skill or artifice.

ARTIFICE is the production or making of something especially in the arts and crafts.

TECHNETOS also from the Greek means "artificial". So you can see how technology and art become connected. "Artificial" means created by artifice and in the 15th through the 18th Centuries

Garden Scape Series #17
1994

16 x 20"
Infrared light film, gelatin
silver print
Kris Rosar
Grey County, Ontario,
Canada

Invention has given us
technologies that enable
us to see in new ways.
Infrared film can be placed
in a camera, allowing us to
record an image and to shift
it to the longer end of the
spectrum beyond red.
Infrared light has a longer
wavelength than the reds we
see. At the other end of the
spectrum ultraviolet is
beyond the range of violets.
Infrared film picks up the
radiation of long waves and
records the image even if it is
dark or there is a haze. Insects
see plants within a different
range of colors including the
shorter wave of ultraviolet.

Kris Rosar uses infrared film
which is then processed as
a gelatin silver print or
black and white photograph.
The subjects are familiar,
of family and gardens. The
images in her Garden Scape
Series are hauntingly and
subtly changed from how
we would usually see what
we think we know. Our
experience is extended.
Often Rosar juxtaposes
built elements with the
plants of the garden. In this
characteristically Canadian
image of the wild, the flower
pot evocatively appears.

was high praise. Faberge eggs are fabulously "artificial." The downside meaning of "not real" is a 20th Century addition to the word. Thus enters the ethical debate of means and ends, the manner of production and or moving though the material to the meaningful. But the ethical debate of means and ends is not inherent in these words. It is an overlay that ignores what the words actually mean. If we move from "Technetos" to "Techne" we get a meaning that is less problematic.

TECHNE means art or skill: the principles or methods employed in making something or attaining an objective. Now all that has to happen is to establish what our objectives might be. As you can see "Tech" has a history, and I am using this to explore the implications of a name for what and why we make.

It is tempting to pursue the root of "work" as in WORKSHOP but let me leave "work" alone because its definitions and cultural meanings are too extensive for the space. "Shop" is fortunately easier to pin down, coming from the German word (ME. schoppe; AS. sceoppa, a stall, a booth at a fair). "Shop" was a place where things were made. To "talk shop" is to discuss one's work, or things related to one's work and finally, a "shop" is where goods are sold. If we look at the tradition of the shop not in relation to artifice but in relationship to the ALCHEMIST and SCIENCE, a rather different set of values emerges. Alchemists were interested in the study and practices of chemistry and metallurgy as well as in the discovery of a universal remedy for diseases.

> Images seem to speak to the eye, but they are really addressed to the mind. They are ways of thinking, in the guise of ways of seeing.
>
> ⟳
> WILSON DUFF

They were interested in the transmutation of one thing to another. In this context we may call the laboratory a lab or labshop.

Language has defined in a rather vague way what we see and how we may think about what we see. However, as Marshall McLuhan points out, "The content of writing is speech, just as the written word is the content of print. ...'What is the content of speech?' It is necessary to say, 'It is an actual process of thought, which is in itself nonverbal'." Appearance of images play a vital role in thought PATTERNS and these images are the MAPS, MODELS, SYMBOLS and SIGNS for perception, which in turn becomes ICONIC THINKING. Iconic thinking involves nonverbal messages that carry the concept of our imagined and projected realities.

Some of the chapters here are about chemicals, or more accurately the formation of materials and their transmutation. For some people this may be the appropriate root for study, the guiding metaphor for science, art, and making, rather than the "deceits" of "artificium" and "technetos."

Appearance may initially seem superficial. The outward look or surface qualities, the solid world or the translucent image of the video image, may suggest something skin deep, or merely a fleeting moment. Before appearance can be assessed it must appear in the mind. If things appear to us, they also disappear. Memory plays a major role in how we see and experience the world. The pattern of a leaf or particular model of bicycle can be recognized at a glance, once it has been imprinted in the mind. The leaf appears, reappears and never quite disappears from memory. A botanist will understand the shape from a molecular and structural level, a flower arranger will understand it from an aesthetic and formal level. Andy Goldsworthy presents leaves intricately arranged in new ways. Each specialist will remember the leaf differently. For the psychologist Jerome Bruner, knowledge may be represented through habit and action, iconic imagery and symbolic knowing. Math and language both are means to a symbol system of knowing.

Some memories work better than others. A highly charged emotional experience reappears more strongly perhaps in dreams or even hallucinations. Strongly felt and held images may help the creative person to reap a vision more clearly. We are each, through the cognitive process of gaining, storing, transforming and using memory, developing our projects and our lives. The artist can create highly charged appearances that are compressed, filled, charged with a latent energy, thus making the work less superficial. Reaping what has appeared or reappeared is a process of picking out from memory what was seen. The creative person will reap highly selectively, juxtaposing to form new relationships and new appearances.

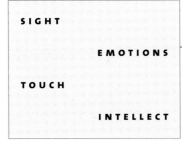

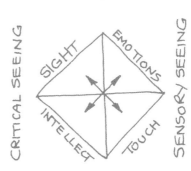

SENSORY EXPERIENCE

The five senses of SIGHT, TASTE, SMELL, SOUND, and TOUCH need to be part of every project but *Appearance and Reality* will privilege sight. The sensory experience of sound to the instrument maker, though essential, is beyond the scope of this book. Touch and the sensations from TACTILE objects will be mentioned more often in the practical light of making. Making is best learnt through observation of the demonstration—the gestural action of the dancer, the athlete in the high jump, or the maker removing a curled shaving from finely finished wood, is best observed directly rather than through the symbolic language of words. The description of the shaving does not tell you how the hands hold the plane, the position of the feet or the distribution of body weight. Neither does it explain the bench stop against which the wood rests nor the kind of bench preferred by a cabinetmaker. And so it goes on with considerations for sharpening the plane and how do you know the board is flat and not twisted or winding. Long instructions are needed to capture all aspects, and they soon become tedious compared to the brief experience of seeing someone do it.

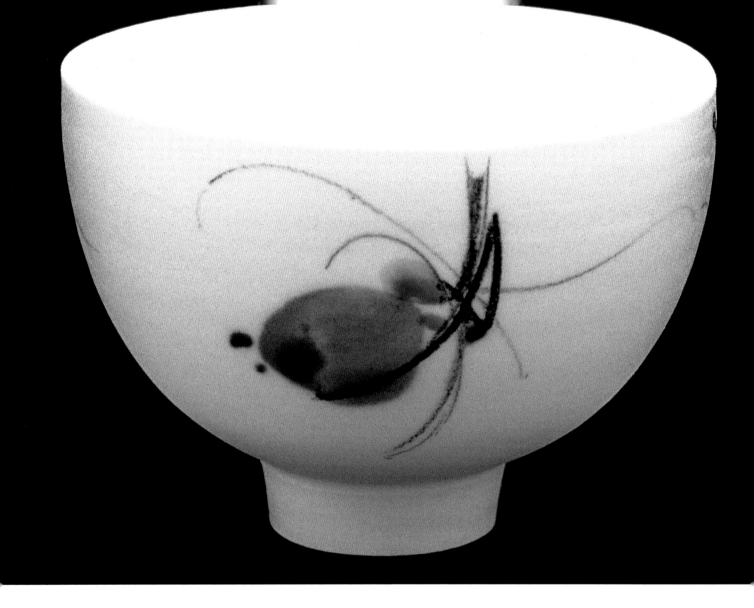

Porcelain Bowl
1995

Translucent Porcelain
10 cm dia.
Victor Greenaway
Prahran, Victoria, Australia

Objects can have the various disciplines embedded in them. The ancient activity of making pots refers to the four basic disciplines of art, craft/technology, design, and science. Over many centuries the process of refinement has been completed and minor nuance is what attracts our attention now.

The design of the form is serene. The spontaneous brush marks are the evidence of a light-hearted pleasure in line, shape, color, and how they are composed on this culturally assured form. Made on a potter's wheel, the work is unhesitating and assured. The brush marks, though spontaneous, are the result of careful observation and practice and appear to hang like a hologram in the dark encircling rims. The colors of the glazes are achieved through the ground-up minerals that are mixed, suspended in water, painted on the clay and finally liquefied into a hard glass in the heat of the kiln. Glazing has its roots in science and in the alchemy of transformation. The aesthetic appeal of this work is how Greenaway integrates all these elements in a way that delights the senses as we use the bowl in the rituals of life.

TOUCH sensations are strongest in the lips and hands. The skin has many thousands of cells that respond to heat, cold, pressure, pain, and delicate touch. Individual receptors do not seem to be associated with any one touch sensation. Touch discrimination is very sensitive in the hands yet pain receptors are relatively insensitive compared to those in other parts of the body.

Makers own TACIT KNOWLEDGE. This is impossible to describe with any accuracy through words—it is a different "language." Some making may carry a conceptual content but often for the maker this kind of content is secondary to the satisfying conditions of working materials to build a sound structure, carefully constructed for comfortable usefulness. The challenge for the maker is not only learning to make but also learning the conceptual language of design and art and how they interact.

What is it that draws people to outmoded means of production? Making does help to connect to the FLOW EXPERIENCE. Being deeply involved in the act of making, the effortless control from repeated actions, the nuance of movement, the accomplishment felt on completion, gives the sensation of being fully alive. At least that is the aim. The balance of body, emotions, and intellect leads to a sense of self-worth, even spirituality, as the maker connects to other people through their projects.

Sensory experience can be highly emotional. The EMOTIONS may rule conceptual seeing. The emotions are closer to instinct—the animal side of experience. It is where the depths of love, hate, fear and the simple pleasures of the body (with a little help from the mind) will be experienced. Balance is required to avoid violence to oneself or to others in the heat of the moment. Desire is both wonderful and potentially addictive. Impulse can become compulsive as compared to the delights of spontaneity. Some attractions, like drugs, sex, and rock and roll, when taken to the extreme, will destroy. Fresh air, clean water, and bird song are wonderful things for which to long. Restraint of the sensory, physical, emotional and physiological side of our nature is kept in check by the intellect, and the mores of the society. All disciplines will have to consider the sensory implications of any given project. Advertising seems incapable of not using sexuality while other disciplines avoid any reference to the libido. The balance of feeling deeply while remaining in "control," or conversely of bringing emotion to the controlling intellect, is learnt over many years and to some degree never ends if you are fully living life. How does the maker express emotions without making it trite or overplayed and yet giving it a depth of sentiment to which the viewer can relate and respond? At the rock concert the audience is whipped into a frenzy of emotion but in a place and time that has been agreed to through the purchase of tickets. Our humanness comes through the mind and body held in the cusp of culture and nature. The self, mind and body, culture and nature, need to resonate together. When in doubt we reach out and touch—is this real or an illusion? Making is touching reality. Making reality is being with the universe and evolving our own story.

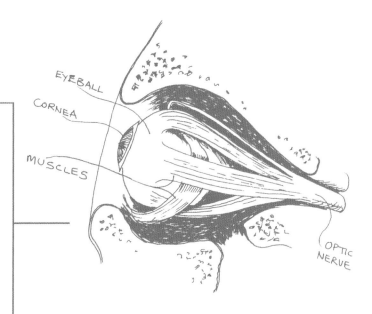

SENSORY SEEING

The eye enables the mind by transmitting images into the brain, but it is not as simple as it may sound—indeed in some respects it is a great mystery. The images are carried on the light reflected from the surroundings to the retina of the eye. The retina is a very dense collection of light-sensitive receptors, which convert the image into electrical impulses and a language the brain can understand. The mind does not actually see the image, but rather it sees a coded set of symbols. The retina has been described as "an outgrowth of the brain." The eye processes some of the data for perception, but the act of perception is integral to the brain.

The image enters the eye as ELECTROMAGNETIC WAVES. But light that we see is only a small part of electromagnetic radiation. Light occupies less than one of the seventy waves or octaves. The other octaves in the spectrum include waves from the sun, radio, X ray tubes, radioactive substances, radar, and so on. The narrow band of visible light on which the image travels is bounded by ultra-violet light, of shorter wavelength, and by the longer wavelength infra-red light.

The light waves carrying their message enter the eye through the CORNEA and the IRIS—a lens and shutter system that focuses the light and image on the retina at the back of the eyeball. The retina contains more than 130 million light receptors, cells known as RODS and CONES. The light induces a chemical reaction in these cells. An electrochemical change then creates nerve impulses that get transmitted to the brain along the optic nerve, to be processed by the mind. The rods see black and white and levels of luminosity. At night the rods work harder. The cones see color and are sensitive to red, green and blue light. Other colors are seen through the mixing of these primary colors. COLOR BLINDNESS is probably due to a deficiency in some or all of the cones.

It is possible to look at the back of your own eye. Darken the room and shine a light into the pupil of the eye from below. Move the light back and forth like a pendulum. After about thirty seconds, an orange background with dark lines like a branching tree will emerge. This is the back of your eye or the retina, where the images of the world around us are translated into our perceptions.

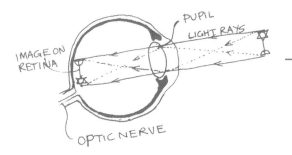

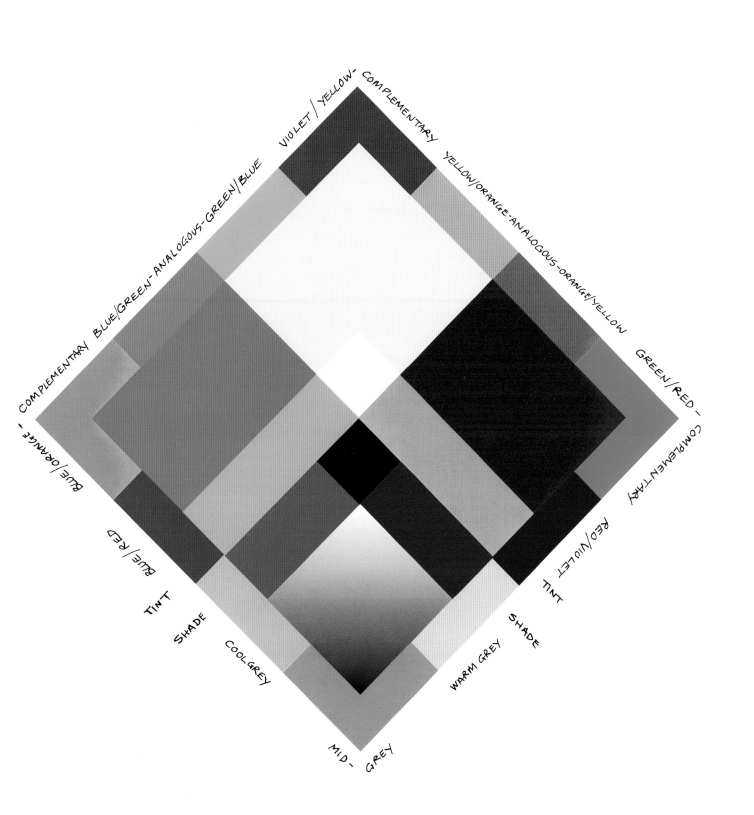

VIOLET / YELLOW- COMPLEMENTARY

YELLOW/ORANGE-ANALOGOUS-ORANGE/YELLOW

BLUE/GREEN-ANALOGOUS-GREEN/BLUE

COMPLEMENTARY

GREEN / RED -

BLUE / ORANGE -

COMPLEMENTARY

RED/VIOLET

BLUE / RED

TINT

TINT

SHADE

SHADE

COOL GREY

WARM GREY

MID - GREY

You see what you see

&

FRANK STELLA

LIGHT AND COLOR

There are many ways to think about color. Various disciplines will think and work with color quite differently. The PHYSICIST thinks about color as electromagnetic energy, vibration, particles without mass, and the phenomena of light. The PHYSIOLOGIST, much like the designer, is concerned with the effects of light and color on the eye and brain. The PSYCHOLOGIST studies color symbolism and subjective perception, in many ways similar to the artist's concerns. The CHEMIST, like the craftsperson, mixes the materials in new combinations. The molecular structure of dyes and pigments, and the materials that suspend the color and allow it to stick to a surface, are central to chemical thinking. However, anybody who works with color extensively will at some point have to consider the concerns of all the other disciplines.

How are the colors within light distinguished one from another? As the early scientist Newton said, "the rays, to speak properly, are not colored," for color is an experience within the human mind. When passed through a glass prism, the different wavelengths of visible light can be dispersed and separated to display the optical spectrum of rainbow colors, separate wavelengths giving the eye and mind the sensation of a different color. It is all quite mysterious to think that the materials that surround us do not actually contain color. We see the electromagnetic waves which objects reflect back to us: an object is "red" because its surface absorbs all other "colors" in the spectrum.

There are ADDITIVE COLORS AND SUBTRACTIVE COLORS. Additive colors are transmitted through translucent medium like colored glass, subtractive colors are opaque materials like paint that absorbs some light waves and reflects back others. Additive colors when mixed together can create white. When the primary colors of the spectrum are mixed together they will return the light to a white light. The PRIMARY COLORS of additive light are red (orange red), green, and blue (blue violet). By adding these colors in different proportions the other colors in the rainbow or spectrum can be created.

Subtractive colors when mixed together create black. By using the primary colors of the printers' PIGMENT inks an entirely different result is seen. Pure light and reflected light perform differently. The primary colors of subtractive colors are cyan (greenish blue), yellow, and magenta (bluish red). By mixing these colors in differing proportions the rest of the spectrum will be created. Pigment absorbs light. It subtracts some colors from the light and reflects back the other colors.

You see who you are

&

HELMUT FEDERLE MULLER — LYER ILLUSION

Computers can be programmed to generate either additive or subtractive colors. Where the image is to be presented on a visual display screen, additive colors are used. The cathode ray tube (CRT) within the visual display projects mixtures of red, green and blue light. Where the image is to be presented on a printer, inks of the subtractive colors cyan, yellow, and magenta, will be mixed to meet the requirements of, for example, graphic designers. In principle most computers can be programmed to reproduce millions of colors. In practice the number of solid colors which can be produced is limited, but the number of non-solid colors, made up from solid-colored dots grouped to simulate other colors, amounts to many hundreds. If the number of colors in an image is large and the number has to significantly reduced for a computer to process them, then the image will become troubled and broken—an effect called dithering.

PROBLEMS OF SEEING

The brain works quickly and can jump to the wrong conclusions. The mind has to slow things down to figure out what is really happening. The wheels of a moving vehicle may appear to be static or even travelling backwards. As the aircraft lands the ground appears to come up and meet us. The setting sun appears bigger than the noonday sun even though we know it does not change size. Perspective on a two-dimensional surface suggests depth, although we know there is no actual depth. These are problems of point of view, or relativity.

What you see depends on your frame of reference relative to the phenomena. What you see is not inherent in the phenomena. It is therefore important not to be tricked by the sensory aspect. Develop an objective critical ability to evaluate as much as possible of the great mystery that is all the mind sees. A simple experiment will help to explain. Place one hand at arm's length and the other about half-way between your eyes and the other hand. They look the same size. Then overlap your hands, and one looks smaller than the other. The effect is known as SIZE CONSTANCY. In a large group of people, regardless how far away some faces are, they seem to remain the same size. The camera with a telephoto lens will pull background and foreground closer together; the wide angle lens will separate foreground and background. Which is the truth?

BLIND SPOTS, AFTER-IMAGES, OPTICAL ILLUSIONS AND CONFUSED MESSAGES are a few of the ways the eye may confuse, alter the brain, and then the mind. To discover your blind spot, place two dots on a page approximately six inches apart. Stare at one of these dots with your nose close to the paper. Move the paper back slowly. At a certain point one dot will disappear. This is called the OPTIC DISK, which is the point where the nerve fibers leave the eye and the blood supply enters. There are no rods or cones in this place. What is not seen at the blind spot is filled in by the mind to create an apparently complete image.

An after-image can

> Perception is the interpretation of a sensation through the five senses, the act of intuitive recognition of the external.
>
> ⭗

**Thermonuclear
Parabola Cooker**
1993

Mixed media
55" dia.
David Baty and Kevin
Brewer
Northern California, USA

Sometimes the brilliance of the product is as much in its process as in its appearance. The Thermonuclear Parabolic Cooker (TPC) is perhaps a significant contribution to people's health and the environment in which they live. How can this be? The cooker uses the energy of the sun hence Thermonuclear in the title. In parts of the world trees have been used so rapidly that deserts are being created. Using the suns energy, rather than cutting down trees to burn for heat by which to cook, the forests are retained. David Baty points out the need *"... to allow the trees to do the other things; we also need them to convert CO2 to oxygen and build the soil from which we grow our food."*

Sometimes the thinking and making processes are more telling than the appearance of the object. The aim of Baty and Brewer is to offer the cooker to communities that have cut or are cutting down their forests, leaving barely enough fuel to sterilize water and prepare food. Baty says that for some regions *"our design is quite specifically a key component to the problem of reforestation."*

effectively be experienced by staring at a blue mark or dot until the brain is saturated by the color. Then turn your head and look at a white sheet of paper. The blue dot or mark will appear in the **COMPLEMENTARY** color of yellow orange. Also try this with green to see its complementary color. Optical illusions will not allow the eye to settle. Moire patterns and Op Artists have both created patterns that keep the brain from reaching conclusions. The brain shifts from one shape to another, making the surface seem to pulsate or move across the page, or to flip in and out from the surface of the page. Confused messages can be created in which one shape has the same weight or value as another. Which shape should the eye see first? The brain is confused by the same value. The pattern may also appear to be confused, and it may take time to "read" the shapes and gather a message.

Most of the time we are familiar with what we are looking at and this can be a comforting experience; however on occasion it can be more interesting to look at the work of an artist. Cezanne said, "Monet is just an eye, but my god, what an eye!" The artist may want you to experience a new way of seeing. It then becomes necessary to see critically—to work with the artist and try to develop your perception of what you see, and how you think and feel about what has been presented. Artists create works that fool the eye. Their painted surfaces are so real they become other realities. The problems of seeing can equally become an intense pleasure for the eye and mind.

> Perception: Act, faculty, of perceiving; intuitive recognition; action by which the mind refers sensations to external object as cause.
>
> ⌁
>
> OXFORD ILLUSTRATED DICTIONARY

CRITICAL SEEING

The format of this book has a sequence based in **CRITICAL SEEING**. There is a defined process by which we see, experience, create objects and subjects, consider and evaluate most things and situations. Seeing is a critical activity. When we see something it is usually absorbed and evaluated in an instant. Is it threatening, desirable, neutral, known, unknown, and so on? There may be a hierarchy of what is seen first and how the information is processed. Before the judgment is made the object has been evaluated from several points of view. Logic suggests that nothing can be seen without light, but the blind would disagree, as would animals with a heightened sense of smell. There are no absolutes, but as the basis of appearance is in the visual experience, I shall start there.

The eyes see light waves and this information collects in the visual cortex at the rear of the brain, where the mind goes to work sorting it all out. Vision is the most important or most used link we have to the outside world, and from the vast jumble of information the mind organizes a coherent picture.

What we see and how we think about it differs from one person to the next and from one situation to the next. The mind is highly selective and makes assumptions. To some extent the mind makes up what it wants to see to fit old PATTERNS OF BEHAVIOR or particular desires of the moment. Clearly, a feast laid out is more attractive when hungry than after a satisfying meal. Experience will tell us what is desirable and what to reject even if, on occasion, the choices are suspect. Logic, common sense, experience, and even a guiding principle will be unable to quell the fascination with a desired food or experience. Habit—whether the addiction of smoking or the regularity of meal times—can also have a way of becoming blindly dictatorial.

When we see, we CATEGORIZE and measure against existing patterns of what we believe to be true. This is a way of thinking critically about the information we receive. Often we are selective in what we see or what we expect from what we have seen. If the image does not fit our BELIEFS or THEORIES then it is rejected or categorized in such a way that we may not see the whole. Walking down the street, a selection is made to guide us to our destination. We pass all manner of interesting thought-provoking things and situations, but our mission restricts any other input. The child tends to see more openly, accepting new experiences with greater appreciation; the child is more distractible than the adult. The artist is forever trying to maintain this highly receptive way of seeing.

The creative person is often attempting to interrupt PERCEPTUAL CONSTANCY. When a car, a flock of geese or a person travels toward us, the mind will adjust for differences in distance and scale. The images are understood as being constant, even though they appear to be getting bigger. Perceptual constancy applies to size, shape, and brightness. It is possible to challenge the mind's ability to adjust for constancy by viewing the change upside down or in a different way. Doing something unfamiliar will reveal another way, or, a fresh insight. Using a camera, telescope or a microscope are obvious ways to see something from a new angle, but even to simply sit and draw the familiar can heighten perception, and develop an entirely new appreciation for what is being looked into.

On occasion we suffer from PERCEPTUAL DEFENSE. If an experience or word is distressing, the mind closes down to avoid dealing with the angst. What we see, and how the mind processes and places an order and imposes its own particular response, is complex. Our vision is clearly only an approximation. Each of us will experience life differently, as indeed we each experience one situation differently from the next one. In the face of this it may seem like a hopeless task to find order or commonality. We can talk about it but the task ahead is to think critically at all times, not with a dogmatic attitude but with an inquiring mind that loves the complexity and beauty of what for a moment may appear as a truth. Is there a way to approach the world that may help open the inquiring mind?

The object absorbs light and reflects back the FORM and COLOR of the MATERIAL and SURFACE. The object is IDENTIFIED and CLASSIFIED, if it is known within the sociopolitical context. The form and material are in a familiar shape such as an

21

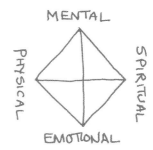

apple, light bulb, building, or chipmunk. Subject matter is established and placed in context but it is not comparable to meaning. Once classified and the context reviewed, we then consider our **CONCEPTUAL RELATIONSHIP** to the object and its subject. This is where meaning is formed and experienced. What does the apple mean to us? Is this a real apple or a representation of an apple? What does the artist think of the subject matter? Is it the kind of apple I like? Am I hungry? Does it need picking? Can I trade it for something else? Will it make applesauce or cider? The apple fell on Newton's head and enlightened gravity. It is a symbol of knowledge. I live in an apple-growing district. The apple is beautiful when left alone on the tree. The ants like the windfall apples. Conceptual relationships can be complex, depending on willingness to open up to the object's potential as a subject, and our own potential to comprehend, appreciate, and express our relationship with the apple.

Seeing critically leads to a more enlightened response to our environment. Seeing based entirely in a single point of view such as desire for, control over, rejection of, will lead to an imbalance or rigidly confined position. Only occasionally will the

singular approach be appropriate. The process of seeing critically requires **DIVERGENT** as well as **CONVERGENT** vision. A divergent approach takes into account all facets, not just those that shine brightly in the light. Turning the situation around will reveal other surfaces that can, under the right conditions, shine equally. This book is directed towards those who are interested in making and will therefore start with seeing critically from a maker's point of view.

DICHOTOMIES AND QUADRIFORMS

Sensory seeing and critical seeing may present a dichotomy or binary choice. It is the intention throughout this book to avoid the binary choice and the potential conflict it may represent. When I come to the fork in the road I must investigate both paths. The crossroads are where the paths come together and it is in this metaphor that I have found the greater insight. During my study of quadriforms I became aware of the First Nation four paths: the **PHYSICAL, EMOTIONAL, SPIRITUAL,** and **MENTAL**. The potential mind-body split that sensory and critical seeing may present is beautifully realigned in the First Nation quadriform—the mind and physical are laminated with the emotional and spiritual. Through time the quadriform has been used in different ways in what may be essentially the same format. Giorgio Vasari wrote *The Lives of the Artists*

SPIRITUAL

    EMOTIONAL

PHYSICAL

    MENTAL

and is considered the first art historian or art theorist. His quadriform considered how some people became great artists through APPLICATION, STUDY, IMITATION, and KNOWLEDGE OF SCIENCE. Johann Winckelmann, two hundred years later, evolved the quadriform in the *History of Ancient Art* to include four steps: LOOKING WITH THE ARTIST'S EYE, ANALYZING TECHNICAL PROGRESS, DEFINING AND IDENTIFYING IDEAL BEAUTY, and THE STUDY OF DOCUMENTARY EVIDENCE. More recently in the 20th century Jean Piaget identified four stages of mental development for children, which may also reflect the four systems of memory. For the sake of simplicity I have found the quadriform physical, emotional, spiritual and mental (identified by Carl Jung and found in many texts including *Man and His Symbols*) as the most readily accessible and inclusive for a foundation in looking at other quadriforms.

> **Mental Blindness:**
> a failure to recognize objects for what they are. Often used of a person who refuses to accept the facts of the situation.
>
> ⟳
> WEBSTER

Throughout my research I have been impressed with the potential connections between the quadriforms. The disciplines loosely align—spiritual with art, physical with craft & technology, mental with science, emotional with design. At first glance industrial design may not appear to have any emotion at all. A wheelchair is a piece of engineering without sensual feeling, nevertheless it is one of the great pieces of compassionate design work that might be considered in an emotional context. The wheelchair connects at a conceptual rather than a sensory level. Within the quadriform the connections have to be sought and discovered in the project rather than only projected or applied as labels. The beauty of the First Nation model is that in order to be a whole person we each need to be open and empathetic to all four aspects. For me this has direct and far-reaching implications in all human acts.

Since the Industrial Revolution, specialization has made work patterns that address only the specific. Context and place have taken a beating through being ignored, manipulated, or wrongly used. I know, I have done it myself, not out of malice but rather out of naiveté. The whole got lost and became entrenched in the pathology of specialization. It is with a sense of urgency that I have tried to invest my time investigating relational models that connect things together rather than tear them apart.

There are certain ideas that will be repeated throughout the text. These ideas are associated with the disciplines of art, craft/technology, design, and science. Each section will focus on knowing, knowledge, know-how, and know-what-to-do. Finally, the quadriforms can be stacked one on top of another. There are ten chapters and 30 quadriforms. *Appearance and Reality* is a representative analysis, rather than an exhaustive one.

Connecting events and thinking critically about how they relate will help makers see their own processes from an abstract point of view. Ultimately, much of experience must be lived; it remains a wonderful mystery.

Grandmother
1983

Stained Glass
25-1/2 x 24-1/2"
Kathie Bunnell
Pt. Reyes Station, California, USA

The visual elements of point, line, shape, and color value can be seen in Grandmother. The depth in this work comes mainly from the contrast of the three main gray values. The white or lightest shapes appear closest to the viewer. The black lines are next, outlining the large gray shapes, which are furthest away. This is generally how we see the work, but when the larger gray shapes try to be in front (because they are bigger) the overlapping smaller shapes push them back.

It is interesting that the light shape or bright light, while seemingly closest to us, also works like a window to the light source, which is on the other side of the mid-gray plane. (As I make the analysis I am aware that I am looking at a slide of transmitted light rather than the reflected light you see.) Figure and ground relationships become restless in the changing methods of presentation. The purple and blue shapes, closer in value to the large gray shapes, remain stable.

If you concentrate on the large gray shapes, they begin to develop depth. If the shapes are thought of as hills they tend to stack in tiers as if going away in the distance, culminating in the dark shapes at the top of the work in the background.

The artist said of this work, *"My human grandmother had a great imagination. The stained glass window refers to her and to the old geologic Grandmother. It's a small offering to the great geologic world."* The work suggests the memories of Grandmother; the colors and shapes are perhaps her jewelry set in the soft and elusive gray of memory.

The visual contrasts and elements

SIZE / SPACE / LIGHT / COLOUR / SHAPE

OVERVIEW

To appreciate and organize what we see, it is necessary to understand the major elements and contrasts of the visual experience. Everything we see and touch builds on combinations of these basic visual aspects. Regardless of the medium—computer, easel, drawing-board, materials of the workshop, found objects, or architecture—everything we see incorporates some or all of the visual contrasts and elements.

THE VISUAL CONTRASTS

Without LIGHT we cannot see. Light comes from an energy source such as the sun or a fire, or from an electricity converter such as a light bulb or a video screen. Light radiates and illuminates other objects and environments, creating highlights and shadows. The sun rising above the horizon has always provided a dramatic contrast to the cool and dark night. What was not there can now be seen, what was imagined to be there has now gone. As the light increases it reflects its surroundings, travelling through space between what we look at and ourselves. Some materials reflect light better than others. They appear brighter, perhaps larger and closer. Perception is achieved through contrast. The way that light strikes and reflects off materials in the environment is fundamental to how we perceive the environment.

It is possible to know the time of day by the quality and direction of the light. It is possible to distinguish between a wall in shadow and a wall which has been painted gray. It is also possible to distinguish between incandescent

25

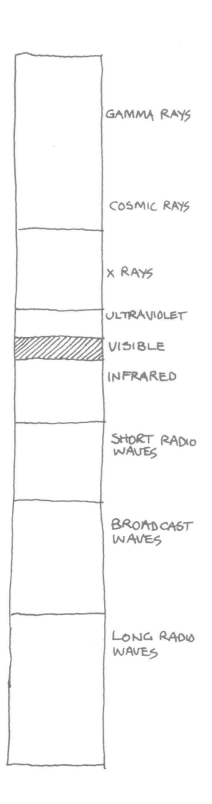

GAMMA RAYS

COSMIC RAYS

X RAYS

ULTRAVIOLET

VISIBLE

INFRARED

SHORT RADIO WAVES

BROADCAST WAVES

LONG RADIO WAVES

and fluorescent light, and to know they are different, without being able to name them or to understand the science of either one. Some artists have been working with light in its purest form. They create places filled with light that are non-objects. They are interested in the PHENOMENA OF LIGHT, space and time.

The sun is too bright to look at except through the filtered atmosphere at sunrise or sunset. A fire raised to a white-hot heat may become too intense to look at. Arc welding creates the intensity of the sun and will burn the eyes. Conversely, although a video screen appears to be a light source, it is actually only a relay station in a complex series of recordings and projections before its image settles in the mind of the viewer.

Light is deceptive, even magical, because it cannot be seen until it strikes, touches, or transmits back from the surface it has engaged. In a darkened room, between a projector and screen, no light can be seen. We sense its source from the particles of dust that float through the air. The light reflects from the screen back to the viewers; their faces occasionally glow and radiate the saturated color of the screen. The ephemeral light flashes as the next image from the glass lens of the projector shoots white light around the black lines on the silver screen. Ordinarily we see a line drawing as dark lines on a bright field, but it is interesting to think about a line drawing the other way around, as bright spaces divided by the dark lines.

Light is a form of ENERGY that is always moving. When it ceases to move and it has been absorbed, it is no longer light. A dark object will become warmer in the presence of light because the energy of light is transferred as heat. Light is the part of the ELECTROMAGNETIC SPECTRUM that the human eye can detect. There are differing WAVELENGTHS in the electromagnetic spectrum that make up the colors we see. Isaac Newton discovered that white light separates when passed through a glass PRISM. The glass separates the light into a rainbow or spectrum of colors which then continues on its path. When we see a particular color we are looking at a particular wavelength of the electromagnetic spectrum. The mind is like the glass prism that accepts the light and, in a moment, separates the information into a band of information.

More information is absorbed through the eye to the brain than through any other organ. While everybody has a brain and can receive the same light, each mind absorbs and processes the information differently. A man may process it differently from a woman, and a Hindu may process differently from an agnostic. There are physiological, psychological, and cultural aspects to the mind as receptor of the light.

There are numerous sources of light that emanate on a variety of wavelengths. It is important to understand the light source, and its effects on people and the environment. This relationship determines how the eye and mind function to facilitate the outside getting inside, or the outside becoming insight.

The PRIMARY VISUAL CONTRASTS are size, shape, space, value, and color. If there are two identical shapes but the SIZE of one is bigger than the other then we see them as being different. Two SHAPES such as a circle and a square may have exactly the same surface area. We see them as

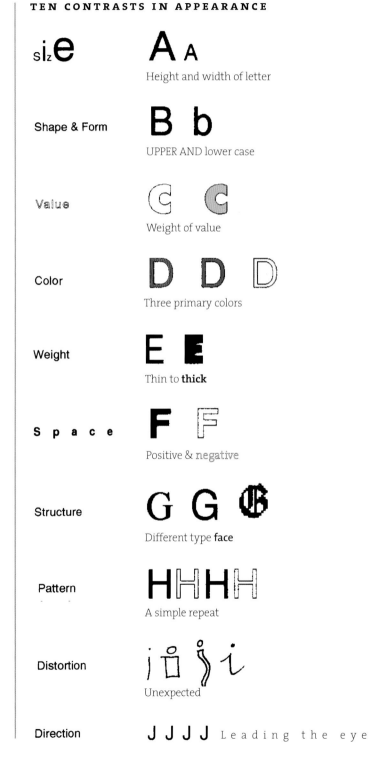

TEN CONTRASTS IN APPEARANCE

Size — Height and width of letter

Shape & Form — UPPER AND lower case

Value — Weight of value

Color — Three primary colors

Weight — Thin to **thick**

Space — Positive & negative

Structure — Different type **face**

Pattern — A simple repeat

Distortion — Unexpected

Direction — Leading the eye

27

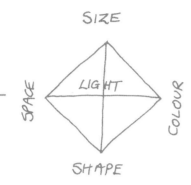

Bruce Peninsular Health Services
1994

6400 sq meters
Dunlop Farrow Inc
Architects; design architect,
Christians Klemt
Bruce County, Ontario,
Canada

Contrast is fundamental to our experience of this hospital entrance. If all the surfaces were constructed of the same material, the building would have a less lively appearance. Points, lines, and planes create mass and volume. Within the stone wall are contrasting points that create a textural plane and mass from a distance. Conversely up close we become aware that each stone represented hard work for the mason to lift and position into the pattern. The lines in the window frames, cornices and structural elements of the canopy offer strong diagonal, vertical, and horizontal rhythms that tie

different because one is bounded by a curved line and the other by straight lines. If a square is cut in half and separated by the dimension of the original square, then the SPACE between the two shapes becomes as important as the two rectangles. Space is as remarkable as light: you cannot see a shape unless there is space around it. Sometimes the space is so strong it seems to be the primary shape. This is the same for a two dimensional shape and a three-dimensional form. VALUE and COLOR make a pair. Value is the light and dark of any surface, which is invariably a gray. Absolute light or dark would blind the eyes so we are always seeing some quality of gray. The complex values in a black-and-white photograph enable us to perceive an image. Color is the last primary visual contrast; it is filled with subtle and striking variations. The pure primary colors of paint are yellow, blue, and red, which in their purest form are known as HUE. Mixing them together in various proportions creates the secondary colors, green, purple and orange. By adding black or white to

SPACE

SIZE

COLOR

SHAPE

many elements together into the whole. The canopy, a plane suspended in space, appears to float, it offers a dynamic point to focus our attention to the entry for the hospital.

The building is asymmetrical and not organized along formal lines, making it more hospitable, which under the circumstances is entirely appropriate. Walking through the building, the natural light pours in at various locations to create a healing, refined and light-filled space. The contrast between inside and outside does not create closure and exclusion, but rather a nurturing of the whole experience.

BRUCE PENINSULA
HEALTH SERVICES

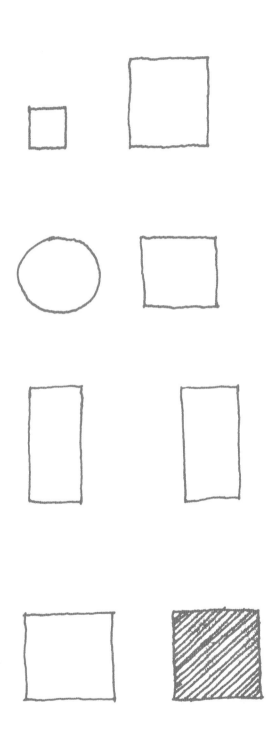

the mix, the lightness or darkness will change. Adding white makes a TINT, while adding black makes a SHADE.

The four disciplines tend to think about color from four distinct points of view. The scientist thinks of color as electromagnetic energy with vibrations or wavelengths transmitted as light. The chemist mixes the pigments and dyes of the material world. The physiologist, like the designer, studies the effect of light and color on the eye and brain. The psychologist looks at symbolism and subjective perception much like the artist, who inquires into the experience of culture.

With this brief description it is possible only to hint at an immensely complex set of possibilities. The text will return to these fundamental ideas, expanding them into new areas.

THE VISUAL ELEMENTS

Pappus in the 4th century AD, a mathematician from Alexandria, saw the point move as a line in one dimension and then the line move in another dimension to form a plane, and then in the next dimension to form a solid. Kubler proposed an even simpler and more encompassing classification of planes, solids, and envelopes. The plane is two-dimensional, the solid is three-dimensional, and the envelope is the hollow form. There are many ways to see and think about the same subject. The Time Traveler in H. G. Wells' novel *The Time Machine* points out that the visual element cannot exist without time and the cube cannot exist instantaneously. "Clearly, any real body must have extension in four directions: it must have length, breadth, thickness and duration.... There are really four dimensions, three of which we call the three planes of space, the fourth, time."

Anything we see will fall into the series of **POINT, LINE, SHAPE AND SPACE, FORM, VALUE** and **COLOR**. To this list some will insist on adding surface qualities of texture both visual and tactile, reflectivity, temperature, and sound, but doing so takes us beyond the fundamental visual experience. Is not a texture a series of points, or a polished reflective surface an experience in the values of light and dark? To the maker the tactile is fundamental, but to the viewer it may well be secondary. The basic series is a progression from the micro to the macro, evolving through space. Imagine looking at the end of a toothpick: it appears as a dot or point. When the toothpick is moved it becomes a line. If the line is unrolled it becomes a shape or plane. Usually we think of shapes and planes as two-dimensional. If the shape or plane could be unfolded like a piece of paper, it would become a hollow box or form. Fill the box with sand and it would become a solid filled with dots.

A form appears to be a solid because of the space around it. The dot may be the same box but a very

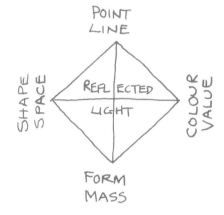

long way away in deep space. Context is everything. The progression from micro to macro and back again encompasses the visual elements. Objects and environments are made from points, lines, planes, and solids, but in far more complex ways than the diagram on the next page suggests. The diagram lacks excitement, it does not create an emotional response, meaning is reduced to a simple concept.

The text will expand on the possibilities of point, line, plane, and form. Appearance emphasizes the visual experience; however, a blind person will experience the world through sound and touch. The tactile experience is another connecting event. Is the dot or point raised? Does the line fade from the edge into a plane? Is the plane smooth or irregular? Different kinds of light on a textured surface will dramatically change our sense of the visual

POINT / LINE

COLOR / VALUE

FORM / MASS

SHAPE / SPACE

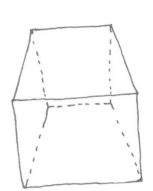

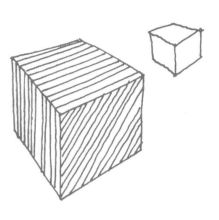

Untitled red and green
1995

Photography
Emma Sullivan
Woodbridge, Suffolk, UK

Red and green are complementary colors, they are opposite one another on the color wheel. In Emma Sullivan's piece they are not exactly balanced in their values—the red is darker than the green. Green absorbs light but in this work the green seems to give back that energy by being lighter, more radiant. The depth and solidity of the red contrasts and complements. The yellow and orange bands create an active exchange with the larger mass and with one another. Yellow and orange separate the complementary colors of red and green in the color wheel, or blue and purple if you go the other way on the wheel.

Sullivan says of her work, *"From idea to existence, fantasy to experience. The idea being the aspiration to communicate, the life of the idea being its reduction, the result being the breakdown to minimum elements. An initial desire and belief that art should be perfect, an ambition to make work that has perspective, relevance, and understanding."*

experience and our physical relationship will change with the feel of the surface. While not a primarily visual element, the tactile is fundamental to the maker's experience.

POINT

The **CHARACTER** of a point can vary enormously depending on its size, shape, space, value, and color. Asking how big is a dot is like asking how long is a piece of string. Its shape may be geometric, organic, or free-form. It may be dark or light or a medium gray, pink, purple, or phosphorescent. The character of the point becomes even more important when it is placed next to another point. Characters and graphics produced by computers are built up from points, or pixels. A computer program will determine the characteristics, for example brightness and color, of each pixel, but not its size, which is a fixed characteristic of the machine. The number of pixels in a given area can be varied so that an image can be constructed with a coarse or fine resolution, or level of detail.

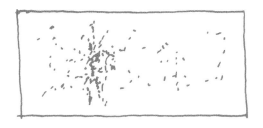

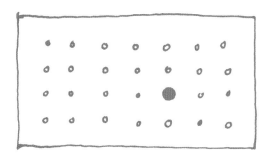

Apart from the pixels in a computer, if all the points in a group are the same then there is UNITY among them. The spaces between the points become as interesting if the spaces have VARIETY. Like a magnet gathering particles, points congregate into patterns from the unseen forces at work. If soap bubbles floating through the air touch and join up, they become more interesting to watch because their PROXIMITY forms new shapes. These patterns are often more interesting to study than a regulated pattern of points equally placed. A regulated REPETITION has its place, like the beat of a drum: constancy and rhythm. The rhythm of the heartbeat and the cycle of the seasons are fundamental to our experience. The repetition or pattern may be singular, linear, in a shape, or overall.

If the pattern is covering the page then it becomes easy to make a FOCAL POINT by changing just one or two points through proximity, size, shape, value, and color. It becomes the one that is different or alternatively the one that is missing. If the design on the page changes to half the page covered with repetitive points and one of the points is placed in the remaining space, ISOLATION and PLACEMENT become critical to getting the attention of the viewer. The relationship between the points is as dynamic as the point itself and leads to composition and the importance of organization.

The material world is made from atoms, microscopic particles, and particles of sand, rocks, boulders, and mountains. The earth is a point in the solar system, one of many in the universe. Sometimes we can see the points or dots, but at other times they blend to become lines, planes, and solids.

LINE

The character of a line can vary enormously depending on its size, shape, value and color. This should be a familiar idea and will recur for the plane, shape, form, and space. A significant difference between line and point is the line's ability to direct the eye along its path. For Westerners the direction of a line will tend to be from left to right and top to bottom, but a person who normally reads Chinese characters would tend to interpret it the other way. Context is everything.

The SPEED at which the eye can read a line depends on its configuration. Place an abrupt curve along the line and the eye will slow to read the anomaly. The curve may emphasize the line at that point, or it will act as the focal point and a place to rest. The line can become fast, slow, languid, and sensual. A more sensual line would probably change in width, becoming thick and thin according to the rhythm of its curves. An ILLUSION OF DEPTH may occur and is easier to arrange with several lines running almost parallel and in the same direction. The space between the lines is as critical as their size. Heavier long lines will appear closer than finer short lines. Put these lines and spaces together and many illusions can be created, from geometric shapes to organic forms. Line drawing is a fundamental means of communication in the visual world.

OPTICAL effects can be generated with visual elements. Line has been used in Moiré patterns, Op Art, and by psychologists to understand perception. Moiré patterns are interference patterns created by two patterns laid over one another. They add and subtract to create the illusion of a third pattern.

When one pattern moves over the other, the third (created) pattern moves more. The Op(tical) artists explored the width of lines and the relationship of space between the lines. Some designs are significantly difficult to look at because the eye cannot come to rest. This confuses the brain and its ability to see. The viewer becomes disoriented. The classic example of a line manipulated is the double-ended arrow folded first one way and then another. The line appears to stretch and shrink, depending on the directional thrust of the arrow indicators.

A series of points make a line, line defines itself, shape and space may be delineated by line, and form is often described with reference to line. Line is primary to visual appearance.

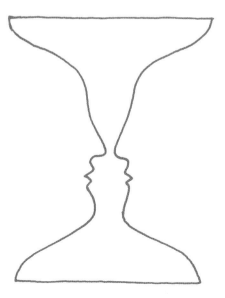

SHAPE

A fundamental aspect of shape involves the space surrounding it and how the relationship between the SHAPE and SPACE coexist. There are other influences and aspects, like the value/color of the shape, what the shape might represent, and what is the context of the shape, but these are other layers of concern. If a shape is of equal value to the ground then which is read first? Shape recognition will tend to determine what is "seen" first. We look for familiar patterns to understand what we are looking at. Other terms used to describe the relationship between shape and space are FIGURE and GROUND, POSITIVE and NEGATIVE. These relationships can be quite AMBIGUOUS if the two shapes represent two quite different subjects. The example at left, a face or a table, a table or a face, can quite readily be flipped in the mind's eye. There are more complex or subtler configurations where it may take the viewer a considerable amount of time to determine the differences.

There can be a lack of balance between the figure and ground, so that one dominates the other. Getting the relationship in balance is critical to developing harmony between the elements. Another kind of balance involves a fulcrum. For example, a person standing has an imaginary axis. If the person leans too far one way or the other he or she can fall out of balance. As soon as something moves asymmetrically to its axis, it is more dynamic and alive. Dance and gymnastics demonstrate this dynamic balance or COUNTERPOISE between figure and ground. COUNTERCHANGE can achieve both symmetrical and dynamic balance. There can be one balance between the surface area of the shapes and another balance about the vertical axis. The horizon line may equally introduce a different axis that needs a horizontal balance. The balance between the sky and the earth is equally important. If the balance is neither vertical or horizontal then it may be RADIAL like the petals on a daisy. Whatever point, line, shape, or space is created, it will need to balance in the space unless the maker seeks some specific dynamic quality.

The shape may have a specific character which is GEOMETRIC, ORGANIC, REPRESENTATIONAL, or NONOBJECTIVE. Terms will vary, as the shape may begin as one type then hybridize or evolve into another. It is impossible to be definitive or objective in a highly dynamic and subjective visual experience.

FORM

Form describes the third dimension and can encompass all of the previous ideas of point, line, shape, or plane. A brick building is made up of small rectangular blocks that from a distance appear to be points. A tree is a series of linear elements growing finer at the extremity of the form, a car is a series of curved planes which, when welded together, creates a form. A boulder is a mass of solid material with the same consistency throughout and is also a form. The space surrounding a form is as important as its shape. At a functional level it is necessary to enter the brick building or steel shell of an automobile. The space between objects will carry its own implications: tight confined space, small comfortable space, open and generous space, the space beneath the stars, the regulated spacing of wheat in a field, apparent random spaces in the wilderness, or the penetrating space in a sculpture.

VALUE AND COLOR

Value or light and dark, color or the spectrum, brings us back to the beginning. A black and white photograph of an egg will show a subtle gradation of values from light on the high point and dark in the shadow of the edge—unless the light comes from the back of the object.

CHIAROSCURO was a technique perfected in Renaissance Italy where the gradual shifts of light

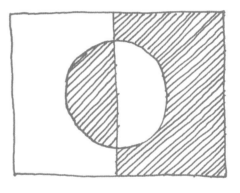

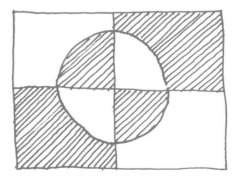

Artworks Gallery
1991

Light Timber Construction
100 sq. meters
Anthony Lake, of Sedunary,
Lake and Partners
Barnsdale, Victoria, Australia

Through the careful arrangement of size, shape, space, and value, the Artworks Gallery defines the regional vernacular of the seaside in contrast to the more familiar metropolitan architecture. All architecture has visual contrasts, but how they are arranged creates their distinctive qualities. Places have visual characteristics, determined by the climate, landform, biota, and the built environment. The appearances of these places may be deconstructed and then reconstructed in new ways and materials. Contemporary and international in feeling, Artworks Gallery still has roots in the regional experience. The appearance reflects building practices of earlier times. Norman Creighton has written, "The use of light timber construction methods and color-coated sheet corrugated iron provide the elements of the Australian country building, rooted in the history of farm buildings, shearing sheds, and the like, while approaching the lakeside environment with the sense of summer holidays and recreation." Artworks Gallery is located near Lakes Entrance, East Gippsland, Victoria and is sited so the first encounter shows the "back" of the structure. The architecture is exceptional from all sides—an appreciation for all aspects of the three-dimensional in the environment.

(chiaro) to dark (oscuro) was perfected. The illusion of rounded form on the two-dimensional surface heightened the sense of reality and the presence of the object.

The addition of color to light and dark presents an even closer appearance to reality. However, by removing the light and dark values and working entirely with the pure HUES of color the artist and designer create other sensations that are unfamiliar and often more interesting to think about. The POINTILLISTS covered the canvas with dots of color. One color close to the next influences how we see, especially when viewed from a distance. The eye, unable to focus on each separate dot, mixes the two colors together and creates a third color. HYBRID COLOR is a term used by computer designers to refer to the same illusion of letting the viewer mix the color in the eye. There are hybrid color files that have been selected to prevent dithering and become "browser safe" palettes. Dithering is where the image breaks down and the dots of color become apparent, making the image textured and noisy. Dithering can be a special effect for some but generally it is disturbing to the image and to its message.

Value and color are influenced by other factors beyond the sensory aspect of the retina, sending messages to the brain. Red on a map may designate main road, a painted manikin or model in a shop window may be a modified red to represent skin, red signs mean stop, and red often refers to an emotional state. But with color context is everything, and the color must be experienced and read carefully without too much projection on the part of the viewer.

Composition

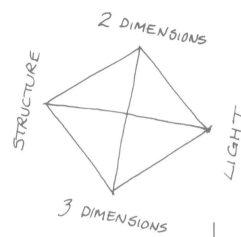

OVERVIEW

To **MAKE**, we put elements together. The way they are assembled influences our sense of unity and our ability to comprehend what the objects are. Some simple devices can create the illusion of depth, such as overlapping two shapes. Proportion and scale influence our sense of composition. All objects have a relationship to their context, and where they are placed influences how we see them. Whether a single line on a sheet of paper, texture and words on a computer screen, the arrangement of rails in a chair back, or the spaces in an architectural project, the object still has a composition in which various parts have a relationship.

COMPOSITION IN TWO DIMENSIONS

Illusions are so much part of everyday experience. Any piece of paper with a mark, the television screen, a billboard, all carry illusions. Most of these illusions

> **2 DIMENSIONS**
>
> **LIGHT**
>
> **3 DIMENSIONS**
>
> **STRUCTURE**

are carefully worked out to communicate a specific message. The designer has to understand how to organize or compose the elements in the illusion for maximum effect. The illusion of space on the flat plane is referred to as **PICTORIAL SPACE** and is created by various visual clues and devices. The way elements are arranged is fundamental to how we experience

8+
1993

Bookwork – rubberstamp + computer
typesetting on tracing + gray paper.
30 x 10cm
Edition of 15
Les Bicknell
Sibton Green, Suffolk, UK

A sheet of paper is a plane
and a book is a composite
of many planes. Les Bicknell
builds new structures and
meanings on the basic
concept of book. Structural
anomaly in the design of the
book increases its potential
as an object, offering many
ways to contain and organize
information. A Bicknell
catalogue says, *"Writers don't
write books, they write*

*manuscripts which happen to
be placed in book form for
convenience. Book Art explores
the essence of bookness—the
time based, sequential nature,
the ephemeral, portable,
intimate object that is the
book. The most complete
book-works have a harmony
through form and content
working together."* In another
project titled Invisible Words,
the book unfolds to make an

interior space with an inside
and an outside. Words
unexpectedly appear and
disappear as you turn the
book around in your hands or
walk around it as sculpture.
The planar form, subject
matter, and context in which
the work is presented will
offer readings not expected
from a regular book.

the two-dimensional image or the three-dimensional environment. Pictorial space will be explored through the illusion of depth and perspective, proportion and scale, followed by composition in the third dimension.

DEPTH

Here are some simple techniques for achieving the illusion of depth. If one shape overlaps another it seems to be closer to the viewer than the other. Even if the overlapped shape is bigger, it remains behind the smaller shape, and therefore further away. If the two shapes are not overlapping but one shape is larger in SIZE, it will appear closer to the viewer. It is easy to compose a series of cut-out squares or random shapes to see how much depth can be achieved. One small shape in the middle of a page may seem to have infinite depth. Several of these small shapes will bring the shapes closer to us, into MODERATE DEPTH, while SHALLOW DEPTH will be achieved by placing many small shapes across an entire page.

LOCATION is also important to the illusion of depth. If two shapes resembling rocks or shrubs are placed on a piece of paper, with the small shape at the top and the large shape at the bottom, the illusion will be of a large object in the FORE-GROUND and a small object in the BACKGROUND. Many lines and shapes that gradually change in size from large in the foreground to small in the background will enhance the sense of depth. If this transition of lines and shapes overlaps in TIERS and LAYERS, then the lower shapes appear to be in front. IMPLIED SPACE tightly crops the objects by the boundary of the frame; the illusion is as if the viewer is looking through a window. Computers

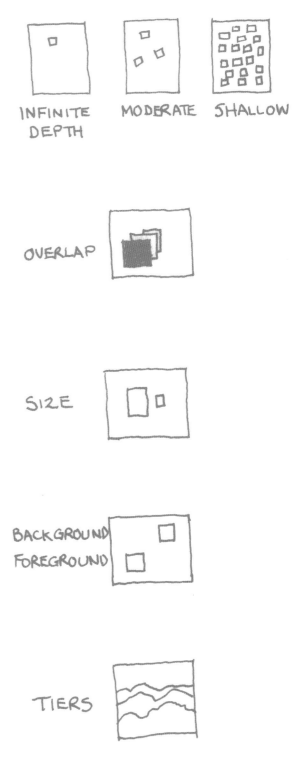

INFINITE DEPTH   MODERATE   SHALLOW

OVERLAP

SIZE

BACKGROUND FOREGROUND

TIERS

43

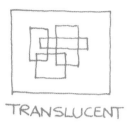

TRANSLUCENT

AMBIGUOUS OVERLAP

edges, and shadows of the lines and type—all of which may contribute to the sense of depth. AMBIGUOUS OVERLAP suggests there may be an overlap, or perhaps not. The value and the color may indicate what is foreground and what is background. The higher the CONTRAST the closer the shape will appear to the viewer. It is possible to set up some ambiguous relationships by not following these simple experiences of depth.

Depth in Oriental art is often achieved through location, overlap, layering and size of elements. Before the Renaissance and the invention of perspective, all two-dimensional art used these kinds of devices to represent depth. Cubist and Expressionist artists also did not use perspective. They avoided any experience of depth by bringing all the visual forces as close as possible to the picture plane. Surrealist artists also altered perspective in the service of dream-like images.

FORCES AND TENSION

An image does not have to be complete for us to know what it represents. The circle, cube, and triangle can be partially drawn but because of our PATTERN SEEKING abilities the mind completes the drawings. This filling in is known as CLOSURE. The form is closed because the eye jumps from one line to the next. Filling and finding pattern in our surroundings requires matching and categorizing the patterns through memory.

Any mark, line, or shape will create an IMPLIED DIVISION of the picture plane. That implied division will make a series of subordinate shapes that we unconsciously read. Once again, the space around the object is as important as the shape itself. Any

may not allow more than two overlapping shapes and in many programs, shapes assembled on the screen are rectangular. There are ways to avoid a drawn box around the image but still the computer arranges rectangular shapes. Compared to traditional means of drawing and collage some computer programs are still rather clumsy.

The assumption in the above examples has been that the lines and shapes are all OPAQUE: their value/color does not allow the penetration of light, which is important to the sense of depth. If the shapes are TRANSLUCENT then it may be more difficult to tell what is in front and what is behind. Perhaps the lines and shapes will appear almost attached to one another. The translucent nature of the computer screen presents the possibility for images that glow with halo-like effects, blurred

shape will create a **FORCE** and **TENSION** within the picture plane. If there are several points, lines, and/or shapes, they must form a relationship. The edge of one shape will continue into the space and will meet up with other shapes or with the edge of the picture plane. These are called **LINES OF CONTINUATION**. They are the potential indicators of how forms are related. If disparate shapes are connected through lines of continuation, they will develop a feeling of **CONNECTION**, of **REPOSE**, and of **HARMONY**. Shifting the shapes of these lines of continuation may evoke an uneasy sensation in the viewer.

To compose with color is very challenging. The tension between or harmony of colors is complex. Some painters will only work with one or two colors plus black and white. The restraint imposed by a limited palette usually helps produce appropriate results. Working with **ANALOGOUS COLORS** helps develop a family of color. To select a palette of analogous colors, work only with the hues from one quarter of the color circle (page 15). To unify the color composition, push the image towards a **VALUE, TONE, TINT** and level of **SATURATION**. This helps give the project some focus and adds force to the idea and composition. Some computer programs use **ADAPTIVE PALETTES** or a **NEAREST COLOR PALETTE**, which may be another way of saying analogous colors. Colors that are opposite one another on the color wheel are **COMPLEMENTARY**. When you place two complementary colors together, if the balance is right, a visual vibration may occur. The effect may be rather unsettling on the retina, but nevertheless may be appropriate for certain kinds of ideas. To

see a complementary color stare at a primary color and then close your eyes—the complementary color, will appear momentarily and then fade away as the eye adjusts.

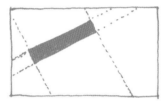

IMPLIED DIVISION

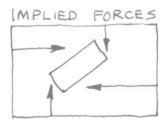

IMPLIED FORCES

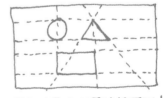

LINES OF CONTINUATION

Scorched Ash Pots
1997

L to R: 3-1/2" dia x 7" high, 4" dia x 3"
high, 6" dia x 6" high
Ash
Stephen Broadley
Denton, Norfolk, UK

There is something quite mysterious about these pots. Made from wood and scorched black by fire, they enigmatically release nothing about intention and yet they clearly are intentional. The scale of the rippled body, much like the marks left by a potter's fingers on the clay pot, interacts with the raised lines of the grain in the wood. The pattern of annual growth rings feels in proportion with the oval forms and the ripple banding. The scale is not monumental, yet the pots seem to contain a mystery. Half a burnt pot would be easy to explain but it is the controlled burn that leaves the question and the delight in the dark textural surface with its sharp, linear, and rhythmic highlights.

PERSPECTIVE

Perspective is a way of representing what we see in front of us on a two-dimensional surface with some degree of mechanical accuracy. It becomes important to understand the idea of a **PICTURE PLANE**. Imagine you are looking out of a window and wish to capture what you are seeing. You draw the outline of the forms and shapes you can see on the surface of the window pane. If you see a dot it is carried on the light wave and travels in a straight line through the window pane to the eye. Complex shapes also travel in straight lines like a bunch of tapered straws. As all the light rays pass through the picture plane they leave a mark of color and value that creates the image. That is why the image of a tree on the window pane is smaller than the actual tree. Stand close to a window and outline an object, then stand at arms length and outline the same object. The size will change dramatically. The window pane is the picture plane. The piece of paper on which you draw is also the picture plane.

There are several different kinds of perspective but the most often used is linear perspective. In **LINEAR PERSPECTIVE** there is a **HORIZON LINE** with one or more **VANISHING POINTS**. The horizon line is established by the meeting of the sky with the earth, and the height of the viewer's eye. The number of vanishing points depends upon the object being drawn and its placement on the picture plane. One-point perspective occurs when the viewer stands between the railroad tracks: the rails appear to converge to a single point on the horizon. We know the actual rails remain an equal distance apart to the end of the rail line. In **TWO-POINT** perspective, points placed at either end of

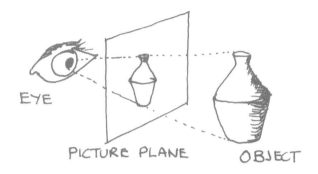

EYE   PICTURE PLANE   OBJECT

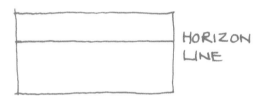

HORIZON LINE

1 POINT

Sterling Silver Coffee Pot
1988

Sterling silver, red gum,
ironbark
26 cm high
Hendrik Forster
Metung, Victoria, Australia

The coffee pot is hand-held
and yet its scale appears to be
monumental and
architectural. There is a
Bauhaus influence in this
work and fine balance among
the large flat areas, curved
planes, and complex details.
Foster was born in Germany
and migrated to Australia in
the 1970s. His recent work
melds his personal history
with the architectural forms of
Australia. Here the rectangles,
semicircles, and triangular
shapes all have to work
together. The triangular
pouring spout points out from
the main body, pulling the side
of the pot into a footprint that
is not absolutely square. This
shape follows up through the
body of the pot into the lid,
where the curving plane
constrains the eye to the main
form. Spout, lid and handle are
counterpoised about the large
rectangle. The semicircular
handle harmonizes with the
lid. Although a simple form
with no decoration, the coffee
pot is quite complex. It brings
together in an elegant
composition functional
necessities and the three
primary shapes of circle,
square, and triangle.

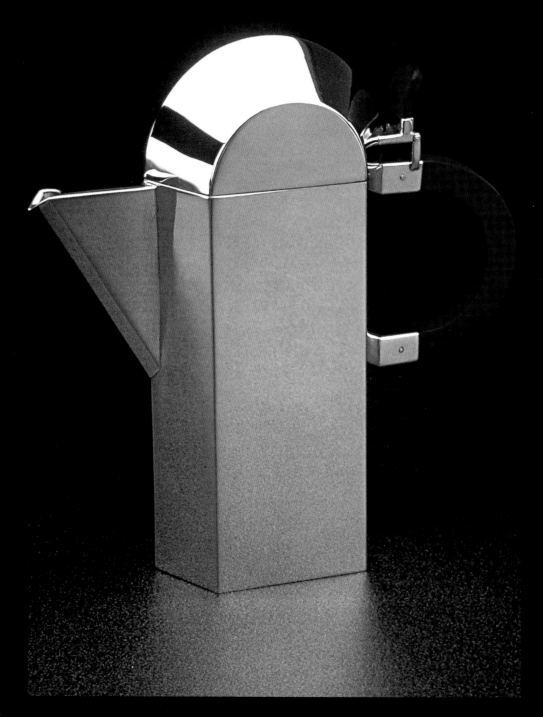

the horizon line act like magnets to many of the lines that describe an object. The horizontal lines of a drawn building will all point to the vanishing points. In THREE-POINT, the vertical lines also converge onto a third vanishing point. The tall building appears to taper up into the sky; the well housing appears to taper into the earth. Now imagine a cube thrown in the air and draw the tumbling form in perspective. The vanishing points move and the horizon line changes, but if properly drawn the cube remains in "proper" perspective.

Linear perspective tends to be mechanical and on occasion should be ignored or used to guide the work rather than to control what you draw. It is as important to draw directly what you see and feel about the subject. Perspective points can be replaced by concerns for SIZE, OVERLAPPING SHAPES, the CONTRAST of light and dark values, TEXTURED GRADIENTS, and CHANGING FOCUS. The relationships within the piece are fundamental to the communication.

There is a perspective view that looks correct and not exaggerated. On occasion perspective can be AMPLIFIED to exaggerate a feature. Cartooning is an obvious example of exaggerating or amplifying a feature. AERIAL PERSPECTIVE achieves a sense of depth through ATMOSPHERIC effects. Objects can be depicted as far away by blurring their edges; they appear to be in a mist. Other objects with a clear outline, with greater contrast, will appear closer. Aerial perspective may also use qualities of LIGHT in which the figure is the brightly lit object and the background is darker. It is as if the artist changes the focus for us in order to draw our attention to what is most important.

The PICTURE PLANE can act as a frame through which we see, a surface on which things sit, or a surface above which things float. Most of the examples have been concerned with drawing the eye through the picture plane. If the size of the shapes and the spaces between them are of equal value, then they will not generate depth or project in front of the picture plane. If a grid of rectangles is laid down on the paper and a darker shape is laid on top, it will appear to be in front of the picture plane. The picture plane can be moulded by the size, value, and density of the marks laid down.

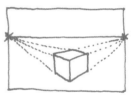

TWO POINT

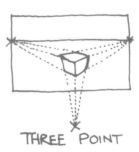

THREE POINT

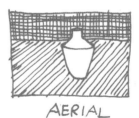

AERIAL

Bowl
1996

40 cm wide
Forest Red Gum
(Eucalyptus tereticornis)
John Woollard
Briagolong, Victoria,
Australia

The composition of this Forest Red Gum Bowl is familiar except that each bowl in the series carries the graphic pattern of the grain and the growth of a tree from a particular place. The top rim is articulated by the tensions of drying wood. The wood was turned very soon after the tree had been cut down. This particular wood was collected from a road widening project. Norman Creighton observes, "These bowls are turned green and wet and thin, which belies the hardness that red gum has when dry. The thinness is amazing, but the mark of these bowls is the ovalling that occurs from the drying and shrinking and the hard and soft grain texture. More reverent than most turnings: majestic like the grand old trees that they were." Woollard's sense of composition carries through the visual balance of the reactive rim, swelling body, and delicate foot of the vessel. The bowl intimates the larger composition of the tree in the forest, and forest in the social ecology of a region.

Some computer games make powerful use of perspective in trying to achieve a feeling of hyper-realism. A scene may be constructed from images synthesized by a program or directly from video clips, or from a combination of the two. The illusion of reality will be increased by the addition of sound and by movement of the images, being partially controlled through the interaction of the players with the scene. However, the absence of subtle or meditative imagery means that such graphics seldom carry much meaning beyond the coarse intention of the game.

Perspective is only one means of representation. It does have a way of making some images very mechanical. Perspective appears as a window disengaged with the subject. The scientific search for visual truth may leave the project devoid of feeling and humanity. Artists in the mid-nineteenth century looked for other ways of thinking about perception. Edouard Manet removed the horizon line and focal point from some of his paintings, challenging the way the viewer would see the depiction of space. Claude Monet painted the same subject several times, and over time achieved a more complete understanding of the subject. Even the most perfect perspective cannot show the changing light and seasons. Paul Cezanne painted the space around objects with the same intensity as the objects themselves. The rhythmic brush marks had the same value. It is important to draw what you see and feel, because this gives the work greater emotional impact than objective perspective. Mechanical perspective nevertheless has its place in the possibilities of appearance, especially in engineering and architectural renderings.

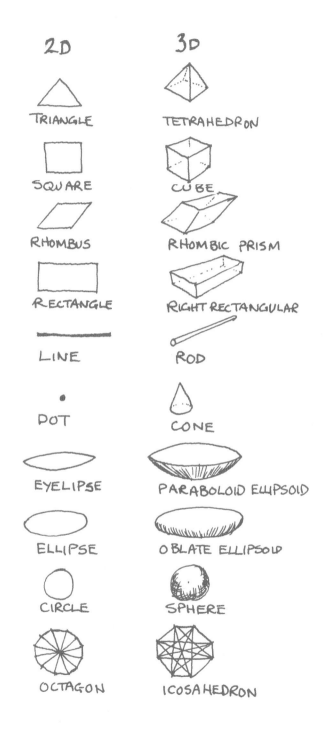

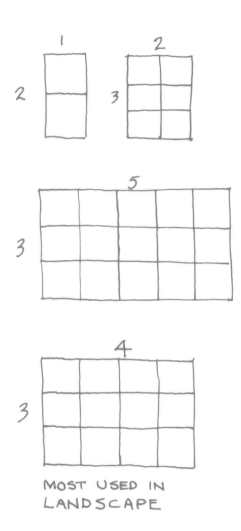

MOST USED IN
LANDSCAPE

MOST USED VERTICALY

PROPORTION AND SCALE

Some shapes or **PROPORTIONS** are **STATIC** while others are **DYNAMIC**. A square is static because all its sides are equal. A rectangle made from two squares is static in comparison to the dynamic rectangles illustrated. The **GOLDEN SECTION** has been a popular proportion since the early Greeks recognized the satisfactory relationship between its sides.

The proportions found in nature always appear satisfying. Perhaps it is the balance and proportions of nature that inform everything. The mathematician Fibonacci observed the patterns of nature and came up with a series of numbers to demonstrate the relationships he observed. It is known as the **FIBONACCI SERIES**, in which each number is the sum of the two numbers preceding it (1, 1, 2, 3, 5, 8, 13, 21, 34, 55, 89, 144...). Many other proportional systems have been developed: for example, the **TANGRAM** by the Chinese; Leonardo's studies of the figure inscribed in a square and circle; **THE MODULOR** of Le Corbusier. Some of these are illustrated on page 53. Most cultures have attempted to devise proportional systems to explain or guide people in their search for appropriate relationships. The human figure has often been the basis for the inquiry. It seems that the search for the perfectly proportioned human body has led to more dismay and display than almost anything else. At the same time, **ANTHROPOMETRICS** (the study of the human form and its relationship to the environment) has itself become a science.

In contrast to the "perfect" figure is the representation of the figure in a **DISTORTED** form as a means to express ideas and feelings, and to represent meaning. Again, the cartoon is familiar example. Distortion of the figure is one means but the figure may be placed in an unfamiliar context. The SCALE of an object may affect strongly what we think of the subject. These concerns all relate to the idea of proportion. Is the object/subject in proportion to all the parts? How can you know?

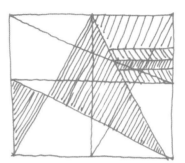

THE MODULAR

COMPOSITION IN 3 DIMENSIONS

3D, problem of illusion, modelling with computers, discrete objects, object relations, enclosures. Objects and enclosures are made up of points, lines, planes, forms, and spaces. Some of the qualities of composition for two dimensions can be applied to three dimensions.

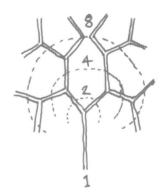

FIBONACCI SERIES

PROBLEM OF ILLUSION

So much of life has been taken up with illusions that the actual concrete experience and physicality of material and form is often ignored. The transparency of illusion, achieved through perspective and photography, and the pervasive influence of the television screen, cannot compare to the opacity of solid materials. Most natural materials have a surface quality that goes right through to the other side. Natural materials are very satisfying to work with, and the results are satisfying to see and to handle. Carving form with this solidity of materialness feels fundamentally different from making constructions and structures from linear and planar materials. Structure and rigidity replaced plasticity of form in the 20th century. Most people only live and experience through the illusions of two-dimensional

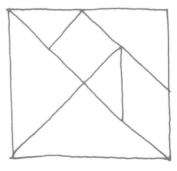

TANGRAM

Sculpture Moving Slowly in a Thousand Intricate Pieces
1995

Wood, wire, silk,
handmade paper, gold leaf
Performance costume
50 x 70 x 50"
Sha Sha Higby
Bolinas, California, USA

Sculpture Moving Slowly in a Thousand Intricate Pieces is a performance piece in which the artist wearing the mask and costume becomes the sculpture. Rather than a static composition, the piece becomes subtly dynamic through movement and time. Each performance takes approximately one hour with percussive background sound, slow movement, and transition. The simultaneous complexity, subtlety, and simplicity of the dancer's composition creates an emotional and mystical response. It has been said that "Sha Sha Higby approaches dance through the medium of sculpture. Using the painterly manipulation of materials and textures made one by one of wood, silk, paper and gold leaf, interwoven with a labyrinth of delicate props, Higby's work creates a path in which movement and stillness meet. Shreds of memory lace into a drama of a thousand intricate pieces, slowly moving, stirring our memory toward a sense of patience and timelessness".

pictorial space and the contemporary spaces of architecture constructed from man-made points, lines, and planes. Kimio Tsuchiya comments, "The loss of (physical) sensation is a greater threat to humanity than world disaster." Perhaps this is why the material-based crafts have become important again in the late 20th century.

At the same time, the limits of natural and solid materials are very real. It is no longer possible to make all things within the narrow craft ethic of natural and solid materials. Veneers of stone and wood go a long way to share the beauty around, while saving many a hillside and forest.

Consideration of illusion would not be complete without reference to computer generated images referred to as VIRTUAL REALITY. Earlier, the use of computers in producing moving objects through landscapes, for example computer games, was described. In the case of virtual reality, the viewer moves at his own discretion around the object and through the designed space. The observer has

> There is an intuitive thing going on, because of the subconscious level you absorb tactile information about the wood. You store all that and it comes to bear on all your decisions, even if you are not aware of it. There is no computer model you can work from.
>
> GRIT LASKIN, GUITAR MAKER
>
>

control over viewpoint and the computer responds to commands that change the viewpoint. The images can be sourced from graphics, though they generally are processed from photographs or video recordings. The illusion of reality depends on the apparent ability of the viewer to move, with some degree of interaction, around three-dimensional space and the objects within it. The viewer not only "sees" the object, but also has a sense of being present within the scene. The technique would seem of value to architects and town planners if it economically enables them to view simulations of a project within the context of the final location. A major concern of designers is presenting the clearest image for the client and public to evaluate. Some people are visually illiterate or just do not have the time to get involved in imagining the project. Even the most advanced virtual spaces do not include the tactile sensory experience, which can only really be felt through direct contact with materials.

Holography is another technique that enables the image of an object to be viewed from different aspects. The object is photographed using coherent

---

Form follows economy.

&

DAVID PYE

---

light, in which the light waves are in step or of the same phase—a light produced by lasers. The photographic image is called a HOLOGRAM. It consists of an unrecognizable pattern which, when illuminated with coherent light, presents a three-dimensional image of the original object. The image is ethereal and translucent, but it can be viewed from different angles. Holographic images carry an air of ghostly mystery which may become the focus of, or the problem with, the illusion.

MODELLING WITH COMPUTERS

In the ceramic industry it can take years of intensive labor to develop a design and hand-model the forms in a range of dishware. CAD-CAM COMPUTER SOFTWARE can reduce this time to a matter of weeks. "CAD" stands for "computer-aided design" and "CAM" stands for "computer-aided manufacturing." Through the modelling on the computer screen, which uses line drawings known as 'WIRE MODELS,' a complex

---

Form follows function.

&

LOUIS SULLIVAN

---

form like a tea pot with a handle, spout, and lid with knob can be visualized from simple outline elevation drawings. Advanced CAD systems will now render the wire models with shadows, highlights and even wrap-around decorative patterns to produce a very convincing (though still virtual) three-dimensional finished form. The computer then can download the information in the drawings to a milling machine or lathe, which makes a very accurate three-dimensional rendering of the object. The price of accuracy with the computer can be the spontaneity of the sketch, as well as the subtlety and liveliness of working directly with materials. The tactile form and the abstract qualities of line, form, color, and the materiality of the object ultimately cannot live in a virtual world. The real world is the final test. Through the eye and hand does the weight and feel of the tea pot enhance the making and drinking of tea.

DISCRETE OBJECTS

The discrete object is intended to be looked at, and may not have any relationship that is functional or contextual. There are three main parts to most objects: BASE, BODY, and TOP. In ceramics these may be referred to as the FOOT, BODY, and LIP of the pot. The critical visual factor is how these three parts work together, and the transition from one part to another. The TRANSITION may be MOULDED, where one part grows into another, or it may be STACKED, where one part sits or BALANCES on top of the other. The way the object sits on a surface can be crucial to how it is understood. A rounded or hemispherical base will LIFT the form from the surface on which it rests, making it appear lighter-even floating. To weigh a form down or have it GROW from the the

GROWTH

STANDING DYNAMIC

PASSIVE

MOVING DYNAMIC

Anthropometry: measurement of the human body.

OXFORD ILLUSTRATED DICTIONARY

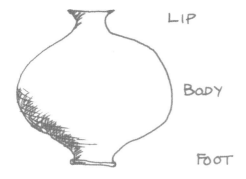

LIP

BODY

FOOT

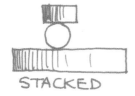

STACKED

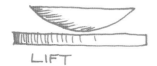

LIFT

surface, it needs the angled sides of a pyramid or a wide base like a tree trunk spreading down into the earth. A vertical shaft may appear to PENETRATE the surface, or point to the sky. A hollow form like a bowl will CONTAIN space, which may be as important as the object itself. These are the gestures of three-dimensional forms; they are often associated with the human form. Vertical forms are STANDING and DYNAMIC. Forms that are HORIZONTAL are lying down and PASSIVE. If diagonals are used in the form, it appears DYNAMIC, MOVING and ALIVE. The difference between being dynamic and alive, and being out of balance and falling over, will be important to how the form relates to the viewer and to how we feel about it.

Aspects of PROPORTION, STRUCTURE and SCALE also apply to three-dimensional work the same as in two-dimensional space, with one important exception. As the object is rotated, or as the viewer walks around it, we expect UNITY in the design. The form and its details should follow through. The back should relate to the front and sides, unless a surprise is intended. The STRUCTURE of an object may not show directly any more than the skeleton of an animal shows, but we should sense the outward thrust of the structure supporting the skin that covers the form. The structure may be inflated and different from its skeleton, like the pressure of air supporting a balloon. The form may be structured like a crystal or constructed from various parts. Form can be referred to as either ADDITIVE (built up), or SUBTRACTIVE (carved away). DISTORTIONS, EMPHASIS, and SCALE become crucial to the object. The scale of a work tends to relate to the human form. Something small fits in the hands, something larger is held in the arms, larger still and it is the size of the viewer, and larger again, it towers over us. The physical and visual weight of the work affects the presence of the work. If an object is made slightly larger or smaller than the expected "normal" size, it will command attention because it is different from what we see as the regular scale.

OBJECTS AND RELATIONS

Usually objects exist because of a CONTEXT. Most objects have a relationship to FUNCTION, PURPOSE, or IDEAS. It can be argued that nothing exists without a context, even if it is simply the context of being viewed. If an object is to function as a chair, then it has to have a relationship to the floor and to being sat upon. If the object is meant to communicate a specific idea, then it will be evaluated in that context. FORM FOLLOWS FUNCTION or at least it is supposed to have a connection with it, but often other factors impinge on this simple idea, such as the preference of the designer for a particular shape or the SPIRIT OF THE AGE. Design is a mental plan and scheme for purpose that probably will bear some idiosyncratic aspect of the creator's personality, or of the mythology of the particular society in which the designer works.

We say, "That is sensational," as an expression of our feelings towards something. The sensation was stronger than usual. It referenced the senses and specialized receptors that connect with the brain. The visual experience is keyed to the PHYSICAL and TACTILE qualities of materials. Hard cold edges, damp warm surfaces, slimy bright objects, frozen metal, plush upholstery, and prickly plants are

experienced through touch, perhaps more than through sight. The sensations of the physical experience are learnt early. As we get older we learn what is pleasant and unpleasant. Memory saves us from holding it, sucking on it, or throwing it across the room to see if it will make a sound. As we get older we use memory altogether too much to experience the environment, forgetting the importance of the physical. The reality of appearance is embedded in the tactile surface, weight, smell, taste and sound of the physical. Think how unusual it is for a person to be seen experiencing something, anything, to its fullness of sensory possibility.

ENCLOSURES

The enclosure or ENVELOPE is embodied in INSTALLATION ART, ARCHITECTURE, and even the biosphere. SPACE, VOLUME, and SCALE, and how we move through them, become primary, followed closely by the lines of structure, and the surface of planes. Moving around architecture and the environment can create feelings of COMPRESSION and EXPANSION in the space. Imagine passing along a low dark corridor into a small red room, then out a low door into a tree-covered courtyard. At the corner of the courtyard are stairs down into an auditorium where the house lights are being dimmed and a screen lights the room with a flashing strobe. The spaces actually change and, depending on the light, appear to change again. SURFACE QUALITIES are transformed by the LIGHT bouncing off them. The shadows cast by the objects across the floor and up the wall are dramatic in their increased scale.

CHAPTER THREE

Expression

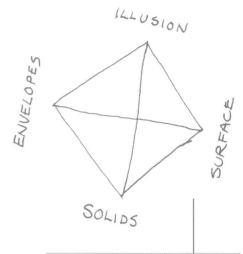

Caryatid 1
1995

Cypress wood
172 x 71 x 53 cm
Eva Volny
Heyfield, Victoria, Australia

Eva Volny has referred to some of her carved sculptures as Caryatids. In 550 BC the Greeks made columns called Caryatids in the form of draped female figures (the male equivalents were Atlantes). Vitruvius later explained that the Caryatids represented women doomed to hard labor. In this series the figure is topped by some other form that refers to the figure in a gesture of pain. Referred to as Tree Trunk Stories, these worn-down, lacerated, struggling figures appear to have washed up on the shore from the recent past. However there is also an older view of Arcadia that is packed with primitive panic. The emotion or pathos is projected primarily by the gesture of the figure, and secondarily by its surface quality. A hundred years ago, Kathe Kollwitz made images with the same sense of urgency. The lack of detail and definition does not objectify the subject, rather it keeps our attention focused on its expression of emotion.

OVERVIEW

Some kinds of lines and images can evoke emotions in the viewer. Light and color—the visual elements—depend on certain qualities or force of mark to evoke emotion. How can surface and solid, structure and enclosure, appear to carry emotional meanings?

EMOTION AND EXPRESSION

There are a number of ways for a project to be **EXPRESSIVE** or to induce an **EMOTION** in the viewer. These include: the way light plays on the retina; the character of marks on a two-dimensional surface; the association of material qualities such as slimy cold as compared to warm dry soft; solids that are threatening as compared to seductive; structures that imprison rather than embrace. These means are primarily concerned with form and material.

An image may also be highly emotive because of the symbolic associations we have with its subject. This will be reviewed in Communication (page 113).

The "accurate" representation of form is often secondary to the representation of feelings, or more importantly, to the emotional response of the viewer to the marks and forms that make up the image. Fundamental to the emotive mark is the

> Color which is the poet's wealth is so expensive that most take to mere outline sketches and become Men of Science.
>
> ❧
> HENRY DAVID THOREAU

```
ILLUSION

          SURFACE

SOLIDS

          ENVELOPES
```

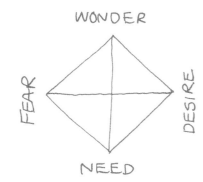

much rational or habitual thought put to organizing the sensations of the discovery. Abstract Expressionism, with all its aggressive markings, flourishes, and gestures, refers to the emotions of the artist at the time of painting the canvas. Expression may be in response to a previous experience or to the moment at hand. Even in larger structures it is possible to find emotive aspects. The architecture of Antonioni Gaudi and Douglas Cardinal seems to contain elements of SPONTANEITY, FLUID ENERGY, and EMOTIONAL EXCITEMENT. We respond with our emotions to what we DESIRE (for pleasure), need (for survival), REJECT (for danger), or we may respond with WONDERMENT for the unknown.

presence of the essential character in, for example, the kind of line: the taut curve, languid movement, short staccato repetition. The energy with which it is drawn and presented will draw the viewer into the intentions of the maker. The ACUITY or accuracy of emotive transmission depends upon choosing the appropriate kind of mark to represent its subject. But ultimately the viewer will encompass the work with his or her own response and there is not much that can be done about that. The artist must find the appropriate series of marks for the experience, and then must work to find the impulsive action that represents the observation. It is as if the artist is recording the PHYSICAL and SPIRITUAL character of what he or she has perceived, without too

LIGHT

Turning lights up or down can strongly influence the MOOD of a place. A textured surface is enriched by a glancing light that creates strong contrasts between bright highlights and deep shadows. Flashing lights warn us and strobe lights pulsate rhythmically, suggesting a faster heartbeat. The strong spring sunlight warms us outside and changes our feelings inside. We bathe ourselves in the glowing light and enlighten ourselves in the stained and colored glass of artists. When the sun casts shadows over a form it articulates the surface, emphasizing and pronouncing the contours. The shadow cast on the wall by the searing light of the searchlight expands the image in an unexpected and frightening way. But then the morning light brings the gift of a new day and with it renewed optimism. The phenomena of light captures the imagination in the most exceptional art.

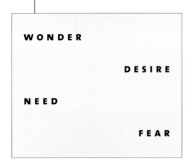

COLOR

Color has the capacity to evoke ideas and meanings. This is called SUBJECTIVE COLOR. Certain colors within a culture have come to mean something quite particular. Red may present the emotion of fear, anger, and violent behavior. Conversely, red may show the passion of love, not fear and anger. Color in itself does not have emotion, it is a matter of what we project into the appearance represented. Colors have associations—red is hot like a fire, blue is cool like the sky reflected in the water. The associations have a symbolic or psychological context derived from sensory or physical experience.

MARKS

A mark may be NON-OBJECTIVE and suggest nothing that is recognizable. The mark may be an ABSTRACTION of something or a REPRESENTATION of something else. The range of possibilities among these three seems endless. How does a mark evoke an emotion? The viewer learns through experience what a mark may mean and empathizes with it, recoils from it, or is curious about it. A straight line compared to a curving, wriggling line will suggest passivity compared to activity. A circular point, compared to a flaring point, may abstract the moon and sun. Some work is referred to as expressive; one art movement was called Automatism after painters who worked spontaneously from the unconscious. In contrast to the dynamic spontaneity of the unconscious or preconscious is the enclosure that acts on the emotions in a negative way. The freely

> I love the mystery that can happen with slowness. You can't do anything good quickly. Waiting and watching are the keys.
>
> MICHAEL LEVINE

formed marks contrast with the rigidity of a grid. Some people feel more comfortable with the boundaries of a regular pattern than with the spontaneous flourish of dynamic marks.

LINE

Drawing as a tool for seeing and imagining has been fundamental to all the visual arts. Drawings of people and the body are central to our history and our experience. The character of the line drawn will convey a great deal of emotional meaning for the viewer. A highly active line will bring energy and movement, whereas a calm and gentle line will become quite passive. To explore the complexity of emotive line it is necessary to EXPERIMENT with different kinds of marks. When drawing use your BODY in a controlled and spontaneous manner.

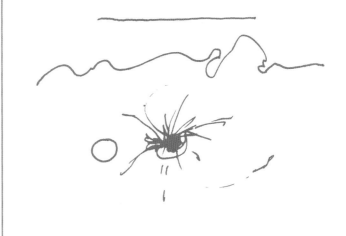

Untitled
1995

Mixed pigments/graphites,
ink on paper
36 x 42"
Kenneth C. Feldsott
Bolinas, California, USA

Fragments of vibrant yet dream-like images intertwine with nature in an expression of the human condition. Some painters present chaos in a controlled and detached manner, but Kenneth Feldsott paints the chaos of experience, playfully involving the viewer through identification with the figure. In these complex patterns,

Feldsott presents his own particular vision of fanstastic images drawn from our collective myths. Emotion is evoked by contrasts of shape, size, and color, vibrancy of pattern, and lines that carry the eye through the work. Each painting appears to tell a story; there is a narrative to be heard as well as an image to explore. Yet the artist

leaves his work untitled. Viewers are on their own to experience what the image may have meant for the artist and what it may mean for themselves.

Use fingers, wrist, elbow, shoulder, and body. Draw on large pieces of paper in dramatic ways, using a large paint brush and a sharpened stick as well as a 6B pencil.

A drawn shape like a circle will appear quite flat. It is possible to imagine that it is a sphere, but shading it will complete the illusion and it will represent a sphere. It may be easier to start with a square because the subtleties are not so numerous. Eventually, however, the subtlety of the emotive form will have to be appreciated in order to proceed. The means to texture the surface, the kinds of marks, and the quality of contrasts will make dramatic differences. A finely rendered surface compared to a coarsely rendered surface will suggest different emotions. The subtleties of the SHADED FORM heighten an appreciation for SURFACE QUALITIES, TEXTURES, and the TACTILE experience of three dimensions. Drawing from life

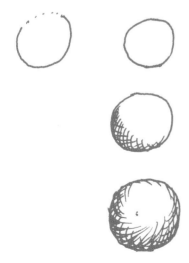

TEN DYNAMIC RELATIONSHIPS

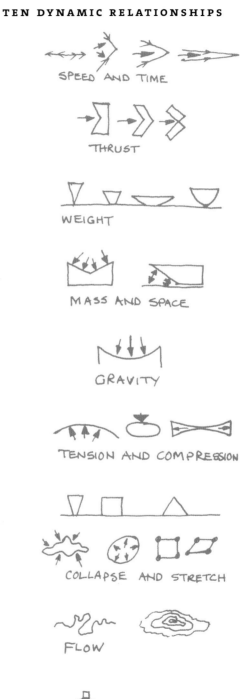

SPEED AND TIME

THRUST

WEIGHT

MASS AND SPACE

GRAVITY

TENSION AND COMPRESSION

COLLAPSE AND STRETCH

FLOW

BALANCE

develops the ability to observe closely. The length of time taken to look carefully expands; consequently, the nuances of form and surface come to be seen more clearly. The act of drawing offers a point of comparison between what we see in front of us and what the drawing looks like. Direct comparison can be made even if one is three-dimensional and the other two-dimensional. All drawing is an illusion and it is a matter of what we make of the illusion. Having developed some skills in seeing and drawing, it is possible to introduce expressive and emotional character. The expressive character of the marks will help define the project more dramatically. The imagination is set free to explore the possibility of expressive lines and shapes based in common experience.

SHAPE AND VALUE

The **VALUE** or tone of the surface creates a sense of **DEPTH** and the four squares illustrate how one surface quality and shape will work on another. In drawing a complex form like the human body it is necessary to understand how a surface will direct the eye over the form. **DIRECTIONAL LINES** make a continuous surface. A **DIRECTIONAL VALUE** will also appear to curve a surface or take the eye back around the form and into deep space. Dark values make a receding space and appear as a hole but on occasion the image can flip to become a convex shape. The light tone on the sphere projects it as a mass. Without a context the eye can be confused by a surface that is ambiguous. Even in the third dimension the eye can be baffled and we can enjoy the reversal of solid matter. The values of light and dark create higher contrasts, which enliven the depth and articulate the surfaces of the form. The articulation of the surface strongly affects our emotional response but this does not automatically mean that a finely worked surface will be more emotive. Indeed, the coarse surface, vigorously prepared, may command the stronger response. Context is everything. The relation of the subject matter to the way the work is created is vitally important.

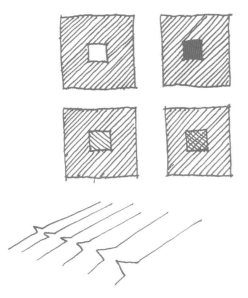

COLOR

COMPLEMENTARY COLORS are often used to create a more dynamic and lively appearance. By placing them together a visual vibration can occur. Complementary colors are the colors on opposite sides of the color wheel (see page 15). **ITTEN'S COLOR STAR** shows the complementary colors opposite one another. For example red is opposite green, blue is opposite orange, yellow is opposite purple. The **HUE** is the undiluted color with the greatest luminosity. When complementary colors are placed together, the hues intensify. Ironically, when complementary colors are mixed together they neutralize and turn a dark gray. Colors used with their greatest intensity will suggest a vibrant emotional excitement. If the color has been consistently darkened and a limited number of colors are worked with, then an entirely different emotional response is likely. A dark ground with an intense hue will offer a sharp contrast and focal point. Context is everything. For quieter moods try analogous colors that work from the same sector of the color circle. When all the colors are tinted the same, they will draw together and offer some unity.

SURFACES AND SOLIDS

Some people are repelled by cold slimy surfaces and attracted to warm soft things. Through **CONTRAST**, a smooth pebble, when compared to broken glass, enables us to distinguish what is safe. On hot days we like cool materials and on cold days we prefer warm materials. Stroking a cat, for most people without allergies, is a pleasure; stroking a porcupine or hedge-hog is done with extreme caution or not at all. The **TACTILE** nature of materials and surface qualities is compelling, repelling, and absorbing. The surface tells us what might be inside. An orange is filled with flavor, an orange tennis ball is pumped up with stagnant air, an orange oriole in spring plumage can get up and fly away, and an orange float on a fishing net will float indefinitely. Inside and outside may be entirely different but there is something about a material that is more than skin deep. When the surface is continuous through the interior, it has a presence and solidity. As much as the wood is planed or the stone is chipped, the changing pattern is satisfyingly continuous.

The scale of solid forms affects the emotions we feel: something we can hold lightly between our **FINGERS**, nurture in the palms of our **HANDS**, embrace by putting our **ARMS** around, stand **FACE TO FACE** with, have tower **OVER US** or be able to **WALK THROUGH**. We respond to objects in relationship to ourselves. Does the material have to be nurtured or can it be handled roughly? Empathy to vulnerable surfaces will certainly influence our response if we do not want to scratch it, dent it, or puncture it. A large solid shape, where the material is a continuous substance, has a power and presence that an equal-sized object constructed of linear and planar materials will probably never command. Mass has implications for weight, temperature, tensile strength. Sculpture in the past was invariably carved from the solid or moulded from a plastic material like clay or wax. These materials were intrinsic to the sculptural experience. In the 20th century, linear and planar structures have changed and expanded the nature of sculpture to include lightweight structures that no longer work with solidity and the inherent sense of mass that comes from carving and modeling.

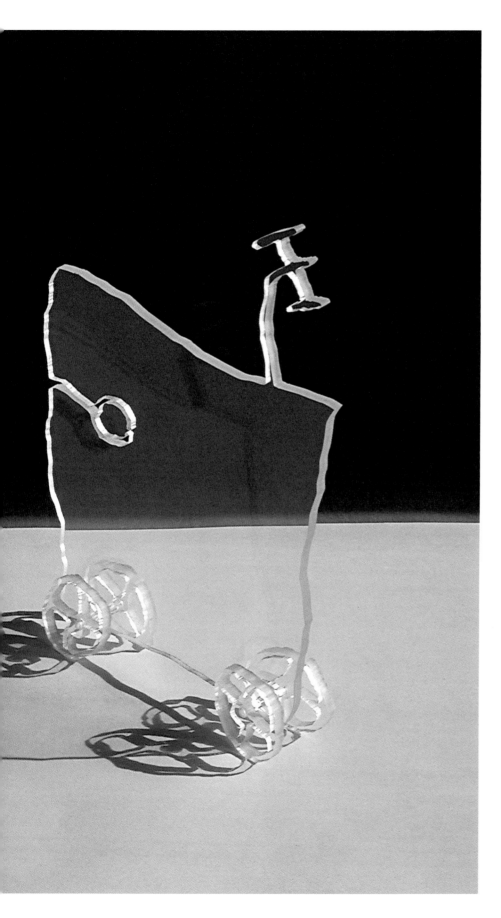

House on Wheels
1994/5

Acrylic. Limited edition #8/10
14 x 9 x 2"
Mark Dixon
Stowmarket, Suffolk, UK

Mark Dixon has worked with the same kind of agitated line in vastly different materials and contexts. Ghost Train was a site-specific drawing in a field, made by sowing yellow canola in lines to create the ghostly image. As the yellow flowers emerged, their color contrasted with the blue background of linseed plants. In House on Wheels the same agitated line is presented as a transient, ephemeral line in space. Dixon cuts acrylic plastic so its edges catch the ambient light. Under the right conditions, House on Wheels reflects the image of its surroundings. At other times the house is transparent, empty of the feeling of home and enclosure. The agitated line and transient reflection charge the work with emotions that represent the transitory contemporary experience. Dixon refers to Ghost Train and House on Wheels as time-based work which is "there not there." In the installation the Ghost Train appears the plants flower; House on Wheels transforms when the light changes.

Bethesda Cemetery
1995

Oil on Canvas
26 x 34"
Michele Carleton-McGillis
Grey County, Ontario, Canada

Vision, experience, and insight are constructed from many facets. We each see differently, the experience is unique, and the way we think about it is our own interpretation of the event. Michele Carleton-McGillis, a recent graduate of painting from the regional art school, has won a number of awards for her painting, has worked as a designer for women's groups, and now pursues an interest in social work. A recent jury said of her work, "This is remarkable work. It has a startling tension between the application of paint (an almost abstract quality) and the depiction of an experienced landscape. We liked very much the tension between the act of seeing a landscape and painting it with a feeling that captures something of the intensity of the experience of being within it. We all felt that an artist who paints with such intensity understands a lot—perhaps instinctively—about the tradition of painting. Importantly, she sees the painting not simply as a window on the world, but as a physical object with its own physical properties."

The sensory quality of her work acts as the primary foundation. Recently she has been painting cemeteries of the region. From the many sketchbooks filled with bold line drawings, a critical apprehension of site is evolving. The land, plants, and tombstones become knit in an emotional, life-and-death union. There is no separation, merely a continuation.

Fluids and gases, while not solids, also have a presence and relationship to solids. Water in a river flowing past a rock can be mesmerizing. The patterns change but remain continuously the same, except through the seasons of drought and spring floods. Rolling mist on coastal waters encompasses solids, appearing to melt the disparity of geometric and organic forms into a satisfying union of gray shadows. The mist from dry ice in the theater swirls about the feet of the dancer as an airborne mix of solids, fluids, and gas.

STRUCTURES AND ENCLOSURES

The megalithic structures of Stonehenge or the slag heaps of industrial tailings command a different kind of attention than constructed forms of brick-on-brick or the curtain-walling of skyscrapers. New structural forms and enclosures have expanded dramatically in the 20th century but the human response remains the same to certain characteristics.

Some people suffer from claustrophobia—the fear of small spaces—while others seek out crevices and caves in the crust of the earth, squeezing through impossibly tight openings into larger chambers. Space can be articulated in much the same way as solid objects. The scale moves from small and confining, to large and containing, to spaces where movement can happen quite freely, to the immense spaces of cathedrals, aircraft hangers, and even the biosphere itself.

Architecture depends on the articulation of space. A Gothic cathedral has high columns and walls that soar to vaulted ceilings. These ceilings and their roofs are needed to keep the rain off but primarily they inspire high-minded thoughts and stir emotional responses in the worshippers. All the disciplines of the visual arts have on occasion worked with highly emotive lighting, marks, lines, forms, color, and enclosures to startle the viewer, fulfill a need in the viewer, stimulate desire in the viewer, or astonish the viewer.

HOW THE "ISMS" FIT

The quadraform shows a relationship among four ways to approach appearance. It is not possible to be definitive in organization and there are other terms and words that may demand another model—there is always something that does not fit. However, for our purposes EXPRESSIVE work is EMOTIVE and is placed with the artist. The way of expressing an emotion is to distort the normal expectations of color, shape, surface, or space in a personal manner. When placed in the context of the subject, expressive projects can evoke strong emotional reaction.

EXPRESSION

ABSTRACTION

REALISM OR NATURALISM

IMPRESSIONISM

71

Gothic Novel
1997

14" dia
Maple and Epoxy
Marilyn Campbell
Bruce County, Ontario, Canada

Randomness and spontaneity within a rhythm that may be found in nature informs most of Marilyn Campbell's turned bowls. Gothic Novel has lines that may be seen as the struggling growth of trees or streams and estuaries to a black lake. The eye flows to the center and back out again along an agitated line while the negative shapes each compete, wrestling to dominate one another and the space around the circle. *"I wanted the sensation of desolation... an attitude of foreboding, increasing the sensation of dark pathos."* It is the restlessness of the design along with the title Gothic Novel that sets the viewer's attention toward Victorian story telling of places intended to frighten. In use a single perfect strawberry, peach, walnut or chocolate changes the sense of the piece, allowing the eye to focus and rest on a delicacy. But perhaps the fruit is not quite so perfect! To present a sardine on the plate would be a very depressing relationship whereas the strawberry is rather wonderful. There can be a playful ambiguity in some projects, in which the viewer becomes implicated in the final presentation.

IMPRESSIONISM is placed with the scientist even though it is usually associated with the artist. Impressionists painted the quality of extra-ordinary light at a particular moment. It was the visual **PHENOMENA OF LIGHT** and how it played on a bowl of fruit or a cathedral entrance that fascinated these artists' perceptions. The **POINTILLISTS** painted with colored dots. When the different colored dots were placed together, they blended in the eye and became another color. It was a scientific approach to developing an understanding of the phenomena of color. **ABSTRACTION** is the juxtaposition of unexpected formal relationships. Abstraction may reduce the familiar to a simplified color shape, surface or space. Abstraction has also worked toward a formal language that has no room for any identifiable image or representation. To that end it may also be referred to as **NON-OBJECTIVE**—it has no function or object. Nevertheless we may have an emotional response to the quality and juxtaposition of the color, shape, surface, or space.

NATURALISM or **REALISM** in representation in this context is the careful showing of what is known. Any representation is a distortion of the original and it often attempts to "improve" or encompass, even possess the original. Which is authentic, the original or the heightened perception of the representation? The emotional response depends on the viewer's experience of the world. Feelings of fear, wonder, desire, and need will come to bear on the context and the relationship of the viewer to the project.

The four aspects shown on the previous page will mix, bleed together, and metamorphose from one to another.

CONCLUSION

Emotions can be coded through specific visual qualities. If a work appears to be emotional in its presentation it may be entirely a calculation of (for example) the advertising media. It is necessary to also view subject matter and how the content has been created. Another layer of feelings and emotion will occur. In Chapter 7 Communication, codes are discussed further and in Chapter 8 Community, ideas relating to the compassionate society are discussed. The emotive experience includes passion and the beauty of compassion.

**Night Sky
(part of the Temple
of The Southern Cross)**
1995

Cotton
6' x 3'
Clive Murry-White
Churchill, Victoria, Australia

The pattern of the flag is
as distinctive as the Southern
Cross in the night sky over
Australia. Straightforward
enough, but as a flag it
leads us onto other kinds
of patterns. Flags are different
from banners, just as a
streamer is not a flag, and
a flag-stone will not fly.
This flag of the Southern
Cross is emblematic and it
flags us to see the other
elements in Murry-White's
installation. As Norman
Creighton explains, "The
design of Night Sky consists

Southern Cross in a field of
forty smaller yellow stars on
a dark background. Night Sky
is part of the installation
Temple of the Southern Cross.
The flag was installed outside
the county hall, which was
the venue of a number of
stone sculptures inside.
Night Sky was installed on
a temporary flag pole, so
convincingly municipal on
its stone cairn that the
council workers painted the
flagpole during a routine
maintenance visit that
occurred while the exhibition

The Curator, Rodney Scherer,
of the Gippsland Art Gallery,
in writing about other parts
of this complex project, said,
"This installation consists of
carved Gippsland marble
sculptures on pedestals of
white aerated concrete blocks
arranged centrally in the
format of the Southern Cross
flanked by two other
sculptures. The central body
of works face away from the
stage (dais) on which a lone
microphone stands. The way
these sculptures have been
arranged gives the illusion of

Pattern

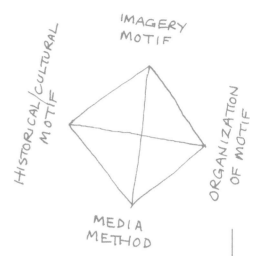

OVERVIEW

People are pattern seekers even as we generally focus on objects. A bar of steel and one of chocolate may share a dimensional pattern but as objects they are quite different. Most people see an object and name it as such. The visually aware person thinks more about the patterns and how they relate one to another. Any appearance presented to us will get sorted into the existing patterns we have already experienced. All cultures have patterns of behavior and knowledge that are repeated by successive generations. The type of images repeat and change slowly over time with new developments. Pattern has a rhythmic beat like the heart, climatic seasons, or patterns of bricks—all of which can modify aspects of time and motion. Some patterns are prototypical, including mechanical repeats and the geological and organic patterns from nature.

HISTORY AND CULTURE

SEEKING PATTERNS helps us to recognize where we are, or conversely, to experience new stimuli. The creative person OBSERVES, then RECONSTITUTES, the pattern into a different set of relationships or an entirely NEW FORM. Observing differences is a full-time job for the historian or critic. The artist and designer must also observe astutely and combine or create variables not experienced before. Some people reject this process, preferring the familiarity of

IMAGERY/MOTIF

ORGANIZATION OF MOTIF

MEDIA/METHOD

HISTORICAL/CULTURAL MOTIF

reproduction. It takes a special ability to create new things that are better than what has gone before. Artists and designers must use their critical ability in a positive manner to see new ways of proceeding, of reworking old ideas, and of knowing when to leave well enough alone.

The industrialized cultures demand a highly creative response to situations, whereas more traditional cultures insist on repeating existing patterns that may be hundreds and even thousands of years old.

GEOGRAPHIC LOCATION will suggest (and even place demands on) the design of forms. Hot equatorial and cold arctic climates need vastly different clothing and habitat. The psyche is drawn to particular locations because of the images and motifs in the land. Any near-at-hand experience that is awesome (volcano), life giving (waterfall), or life threatening (precipice) is likely to appear in the myths, and in the work produced collectively and individually.

IMAGERY AND MOTIF

The selection of an image may be given to the maker through the stories of a culture or more directly through the immediate requirements of the project at hand, or even by the client. If the maker is accustomed to receiving instructions about the form in the work, it becomes difficult to envision a new appearance. A maker practiced in developing forms and who has a vocabulary of motifs will more readily see new relationships and patterns. Some people tend to be more receptive when working for others, while others are proactive, forging their own visions.

ICONIC IMAGES

An icon is a pictorial representation of a subject. Iconic images have different functions and can be categorized as MAPS, MODELS, SIGNS, and SYMBOLS. MAPS try to give a factual account through careful measurement. Most of the time, the cartographer makes every attempt for accuracy. Maps may include signs and symbols but these too must conform to the collective thinking patterns. MODELS are life-like but selective. The process of selectivity helps to qualify what the model represents. Emphasis in a cartoon models the essential characteristics of the person. SIGNS are substitutes for words. Each of these signs + T # * is an icon that can be read to mean addition, highway junction, number, or star. But if you work for the Red Cross the + symbol is more likely to be seen as the icon for the organization, and if you work for a manufacturer of steel the T will refer to the familiar hot-rolled tee bar cross section. SYMBOLS allude to meaning. The symbolized image refers to inward sensation or experience. Outward observation and factual accuracy are less important.

Metamorphosis: Change of form, esp. magic transformation as of a person into a beast or plant etc. ; changed form; change of character, circumstance, etc. ; (zool.) change, usually rapid, between immature form and adult.

☙

OXFORD ILLUSTRATED DICTIONARY

ORGANIZATION OF MOTIF

Any REPETITION or RHYTHM will place us in the time frame of our heartbeat, of the changing seasons, of music, and so on. Movement takes time and time is movement. Rhythm can be CONTINUOUS, ALTERNATING, PROGRESSIVE or RADIATING. A continuous rhythm can start as a passive reassuring beat but it will eventually become a noise and an irritation. The single rhythm can change, MODULATING and enriching what we see. The point, line, or shape evolves—expanding, shrinking, pulsating, and bending—into subtle, alternating, or progressive contrasts. The sense of time can be increased or decreased by the proximity and density of the visual elements. The rhythm can be fine, heavy, slow, languid, fast, or directional. Placed together these dynamic properties of rhythm can mean absolute CHAOS. Even a simple movement can force the eye to keep moving in a restless manner.

The most understood pattern is the straightforward repeating pattern. The REGULATED REPEAT patterns of brick wall, paving stone, or wallpaper are most familiar. There are PATTERNS OF CHANCE that appear as random marks or arrangements. Some would argue that because of cause and effect there is no such thing as chance. Within natural phenomena this will happen but the human imagination can see new relationships by juxtaposing unexpected relationships. The chance encounter has often proven of considerable interest to the creative mind. Physics is involved in any material event and the event will be determined by the nature of materials in their context. CHAOS THEORY explains that there is always a sensitive dependence on the initial condition. The chaotic

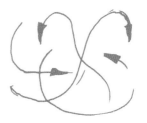

Orfordness
1994

Line etching and aquatint,
printing in six colors from one plate.
40 x 26 x 5 cm
Glynn Thomas
Ipswich, Suffolk, UK

The familiar forms, structures, and spatial relations are reconfigured into a new pattern in Glynn Thomas' etching. Still familiar, we see the place; with a fresh vision it becomes a new appearance. While there is still evidence of perspective, the spatial arrangement in Orfordness is influenced by oriental composition. Overlaps, placement, and size are as important as vanishing points. The multiplicity of viewpoints also has precedence in Cubism, but Thomas has evolved his own particular patterns for seeing the familiar.

pattern of cumulus clouds evolves within a frame of reference and it is only the imagination that can see something other than the physics of cloud evolution. TRANSFORMATIVE PATTERNS, for example of the egg to chrysalis to butterfly, suggests the patterns of living things. These patterns metamorphose, grow, expand, regenerate, and decay. They transfix us with their movement from one condition to another.

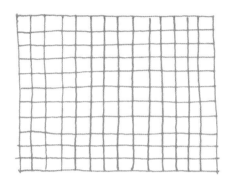

IMPLIED MOVEMENT

Movement can also be achieved through a BLURRED EDGE, LACK OF CLEAR OUTLINES or an INCOMPLETE SHAPE. The eye or, more correctly, the memory, fills in the missing elements. It passes by so rapidly the entire form is not apprehended. OVERLAPPING and TRANSPARENCY can also create a sense of movement. In two-dimensional space the illusion can be seen to move across the picture plane or back into deep space. Visual movement and memory are irrefutably linked. If the image is not balanced then it appears unstable and movement is imminent. The sensation of falling, or the influence of GRAVITY on all our actions, affects how we see the image.

A repetitive image in a changing relationship can represent a revolving or falling form. The rhythm of PROGRESSING SHAPES will animate a form. PATTERNS OF GROWTH extend the shape from one form to another. A METAMORPHOSIS takes place: the larvae becomes a chrysalis becomes a butterfly and continues to TRANSFORM. The shape distorts, the scale evolves, the contrasts subtly draw the viewer along the NARRATIVE of form.

DAZZLE IN PATTERN

Patterns start as a single element, add more and a REPEAT THROUGH SEVERAL WILL OCCUR, then a REPEAT THROUGH NUMEROUS until the repeating element appears as a REPEAT THROUGH TEXTURE. Within this range, repeats that are numerous or textural may produce a dazzle effect. To reduce a dazzle, establish a hierarchy of one line over another. Through controlling the contrast of size, shape, value, and color, a reduced or increased dazzle can be achieved. The OP (optical) ARTISTS used these phenomena to great effect in their work. The eye becomes confused by the image and cannot

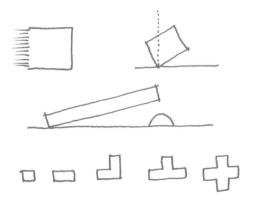

determine which element is more important—the space between the lines has the same value as the line itself. This can produce a dazzling sense of movement when actually there is no movement at all.

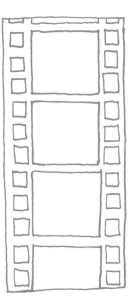

ACTUAL MOVEMENT

Film exists on the borderline between being a moving image or a static image. Each frame of the film is a static image, but when passed through a camera at 30 frames per second, the images appear to move across the screen. Is it actually moving or is it static? Take it whichever way you prefer. A **MOBILE** rotates and presents different relationships among its suspended forms. The movement may be powered by a motor or by the energy of the wind. Many objects are designed to move through space and will in turn have moving parts. The fact that they have to move will influence their form, for example, to aerodynamically lift the plane into the air. But aerodynamically designed metal forms are crude compared to the subtlety of a living bird.

TIME AND MOVEMENT through space are fundamental to the experience of art installations, architecture, and the environment. To move about we need to exercise our memory and follow a prescribed path, discover new routes, or just stroll around. The movement of the body affects the

Mobile: a form of abstract sculpture which aims to depict movement i.e., kinetic rather than static rhythms as by an arrangement of thin forms, rings, rods, etc., suspended in mid-air by fine wires.

OXFORD ILLUSTRATED DICTIONARY

viewer deeply: whether climbing stairs or a rock face; feeling the different surfaces of gravel, turf, concrete, mud or stone; or turning the corner into another space. Our own movement may be stressed, relaxed, racing, or just sitting quietly while contemplating the experience of others moving. The sensation of movement and how places are experienced will strongly affect how we think and emotionally respond to images and to the spaces through which we move.

MEDIA AND METHOD

INCESSANT REPETITION strengthens the weak image, think of Warhol soup cans, or conversely, repetition trivializes a strong image, think of the Mona Lisa, endless poor reproductions of a great work of art. These generalities may not be entirely true and each situation must be thought about critically. A single building brick on its own generally has little importance but when many are placed together to become repeating elements in architecture, great spatial forms can be created. The sum is greater than the parts. Sometimes the way the repeating elements are put together gathers much of our attention. The great stones of Machu Picchu architecture, their complex and precise cut and ground forms, are fascinating to anybody who has worked with similar materials. The repeating elements all vary from one block to the next.

For want of a nail,
the shoe was lost
For want of a shoe,
the horse was lost
For want of a horse,
the rider was lost...
↔

Loose type and the Gutenberg press enabled the reproduction of a single image over and over again. It enabled a radical shift in the production of images and was the start of mass communication. The Victorian public, enthused by the possibility of pattern, excessively covered everything and consequently pattern lost much of its potential meaning. William Morris, so offended by these excesses, reduced many of his designs to their essential forms while printing wonderful wallpaper patterns in his own workshop. Artists still pursued pattern in paintings. Georges Seurat, Pointillism, and later Henri Matisse, Gustav Klimt, and many other artists produced highly patterned works. As the Industrial Revolution got underway and methods of production improved, pattern was superseded by the potential of mass production and the aesthetics of structural designs. The bentwood furniture of Michael Thonet became a model for modern structural forms. Some designers spoke out vehemently against pattern, even seeing it as a crime. Today pattern can still be seen in all disciplines but much of the early insight, feeling and meanings of pattern seems difficult to pursue in the context of either Modernism or consumerism.

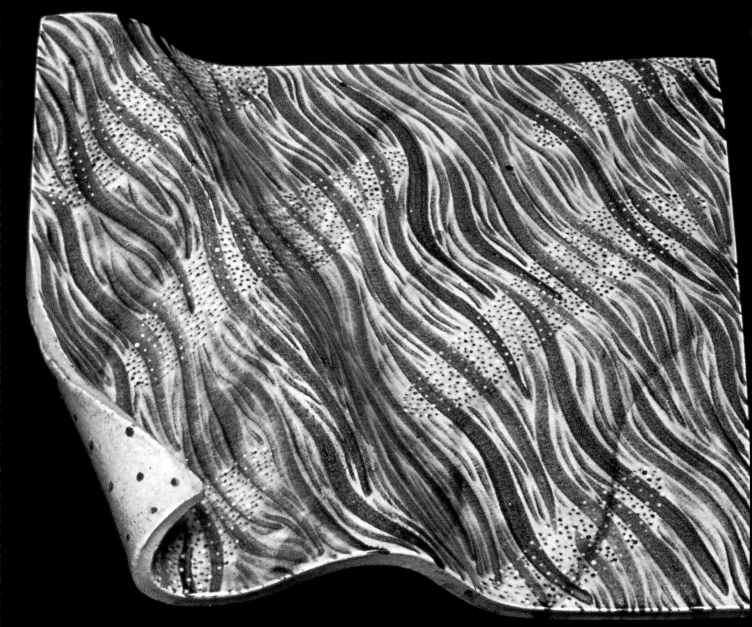

Plate
1992

Ceramic
19 x 19 x 2-1/2"
Rick Yoshimoto
Inverness, California, USA

A slab of clay curls, undulates, and ripples, drawing the eye into the depths of ever finer lines. One moment the plate is a "window" looking into the water, the next it is a solid and physical object showing yet another pattern on its underside. The patterns are two-dimensional and three-dimensional. The two-dimensional illusion on the flat plane works with pictorial space. The size of lines and placement of the texture of dots creates a patterned shape that is woven together by the lines. The eye is drawn into the depths through lines decreasing in size. The texture of dots with their corresponding lines develops a rippling current in one direction while the actual physical ripple in the clay slab travels in the other direction. Under-currents and rippling surfaces interact gently with one another. The illusion of the window through which we look is interrupted by the turned corner, which returns the work to an entirely physical object. The dots on the back or underside draw the eye and hand to turn the piece, because the mystery of top to underside needs investigation. It is an involving and evolving work which, through pattern, draws one into fundamental and interrelated rhythms of experience.

PATTERNS FROM NATURE

The patterns of nature seem diverse and endless but there are elementary PROTOTYPICAL PATTERNS that form a basis for understanding the appearance of nature. Most patterns are the result of stress produced through growth or erosion. The pattern worn by erosion often reveals the initial pattern of growth. These growth patterns show how things evolved toward a configuration of the FITTEST FORM using the LEAST ENERGY.

FRACTALS

FRACTALS are progressive patterns. The word "fractal" comes from *fractus*—Latin for broken. Within the basic pattern of fractals there can be enormous variety. No two clouds are the same, or leaves on a tree, or rivers, fantastic shells, or people. Fractals in nature are three-dimensional but computer generated images that use the essential principles of fractals are represented two-dimensionally. The principle works because by taking a simple element

2D

SPIRALS

MEANDERS

RADIATING

BRANCHING

CRACKING

3D

HELIXES

TANGLES

EXPLOSIONS

SPACE FILLER

PACKING

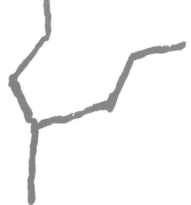

Green Fish
1992/3

84 x 41 x 10 cm
Clay
Jim Hong Louie
Grey County, Ontario, Canada

Green Fish is striking not only at a sensory level with the dramatically contrasting pattern of the skeletal structure against the form of the fish, but also at a conceptual level with patterns of life-death cycles in nature. Jim Hong Louie says his interests in death are in the traditions of Mexican and Chinese art, which celebrate patterns of life in all their diversity.

While the concept was informed by Canadian fishery problems, Louie notes that in the Owen Sound district of Lake Huron the return of the fish to spawn and die will be projectively seen in the work, as genetically engineered salmon finally are presented on the dinner plate.

The fish, on closer inspection, is a composite of various species, adding to the range of interpretation and to our conceptual relation with the work. In this evocative work it seems inevitable that the patterns appear dined on, X-rayed, and presented as both terrible and beautiful.

and continuing to repeat it, building all the time on the previous element, an ORGANIC PATTERN emerges. Trees or ferns have fractal patterns where a trunk becomes a branch and then a twig, and it looks the same at every magnification. Unlike a tree the scale of a fractal is theoretically infinite—it can continue to grow indefinitely. Within the design there is a turbulence where all things are flowing while remaining the same. Fractals are bound to the simple idea of ITERATION—that is, the same unit is continuously repeated. The element is iterated or repeated many times and what is interesting is the SELF-SIMILARITY of the small pattern to the big pattern. The pattern of the fern contains smaller yet similar patterns. The next stage of fractals is the idea of REPLACEMENT. If you take a line and divide it into three equal parts —+—+— then add a fourth line the same length as the three equal parts, a new figure emerges. —⌃— When this rule is applied to a triangle, a star is born. ✡

> "... a man's work is nothing but this slow trek to rediscover, through the detour of art, those two or three great and simple images in whose presence his heart first opened. "
>
> ⌇
> **ALBERT CANNS ON INNOVATION**
> THE REBIRTH OF NATURE

> Once is an instance. Twice maybe an accident. But three times or more makes a pattern.
>
> ⌇
> **DIANE ACKERMAN**

> By continuing to apply the replacement rule and iterating the figure a Von Koch snowflake forms.
>
> ⌇
> **MICHAEL MCGUIRE**
> AN EYE FOR FRACTALS

CONCLUSION

Pattern has been presented in many forms, including the invented patterns of people from diverse cultures; the theoretical maps and models from conceptualization; the movement that can be created from patterns; the cultural patterns of type, Pointillism, wallpaper, bricks in a wall, or Warhol paint cans; the construct of science representing via fractals the formal patterns of nature. To this may be added the transition from pattern to texture. Texture, the smallest of repeating patterns, delights the eye, fingertips, and feet. How dull the world would be without tactile textures. Perhaps everything has texture, from the coarsest of surfaces to the atomic building blocks of the material world. Reading the surface may be highly sensual and intellectual, as powerfully seen through the texture and pattern of Braille. The raised letters of Braille offer the visually impaired insight through the tactile, transferring their reality of pattern through the touch of fingertips to the mind.

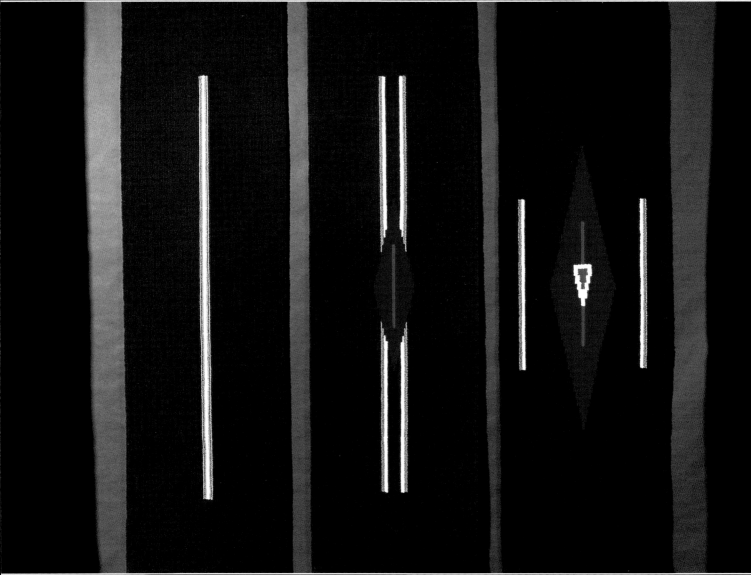

CHAPTER FIVE

Rite of Passage
1995

Wool, silk, rayon cord
3 panels each 60 x 200 cm
Ann Greenwood
Darlimurla, Victoria, Australia

The fabric is made from a single thickness line, using different colors. This line, when woven, transforms into a design of lines, shapes, and spaces. The design shows a visual transformation. It presents another way to think about transformation. What is happening visually? There is sequence and transition within the design. If the piece is viewed from right to left, the pattern of lines and shapes implodes. The sequence moves toward an imaginary fourth panel that would be just black. If we view the work the other way, from left to right, the sequence explodes. The design expands from one line that splits into two with a red diamond shape at its center. In the last panel lines reduce in length and move apart as the center red and white star increases in size. The fourth panel we imagine will progressively transform—but to what? Turn the image on its side and we tend to read it differently—how does the orientation influence the transition? The image and the three panels can be placed in either a descending pattern into the earth, or an ascending pattern into the night sky. The simplicity of the design and its transformation give the work a transcendent quality. The piece is a metaphor for transformation and personal insight.

Transformation

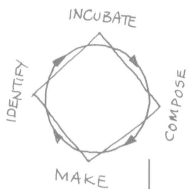

OVERVIEW

We can view the subject of **TRANSFORMATION AND CREATIVITY** from each of the four disciplines and their traditional working methods. Creativity and problem solving have become separate disciplines where strategies for transformation have been identified and honed. However, you will find that the four approaches are still in general use. Often more than one approach will be followed by people trained in any one discipline. When more than one method is applied, the results are likely to contain a deeper understanding of and appreciation for the project.

MULTIPLE INTELLIGENCE

In the last section, making contrasts and composing them in two and three dimensions was analyzed. Why is it that some people have a greater facility for arranging, rearranging, and inventing new visual experiences? It is in part physiological and psychological factors, and in part the environment in which a person works. Some people's minds are smarter, some are more practiced, and others are more open to new possibilities. A high **INTELLIGENCE** does not automatically make one a great designer or artist; nevertheless,

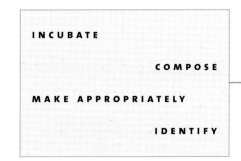

INCUBATE

COMPOSE

MAKE APPROPRIATELY

IDENTIFY

the complexity of designing an aircraft as compared to a ceramic bowl will require different levels of ability. Both tasks can be approached creatively, though one is more complex than the other. The simple bowl, so familiar after thousands of years of development and refinement, can be more difficult to re-invent than a new form derived from material or technological innovation.

How can the **COMPUTER** be used in the process of creativity and transformation? The computer may be used in some projects to aid in problem-solving as well as in the realization of the solution. Computers help us cope with complexity. A computer is a sophisticated calculator, an image processor, memory storage with easy and reliable access, or a grammar-and-spelling checker—all terribly useful tasks. But computers cannot actually solve problem unless someone is correctly typing on the keyboard, moving and clicking the mouse accurately, and more importantly, thinking about the project. Computers come into their own when dealing with complexity. Architecture with curved walls can be drawn and presented with vastly greater ease than via traditional forms of drawing. Some weavers use the computer for pattern development, bypassing the tedium of drafting repeats. Potters use computers to chart their way through many complex variations in glaze formulas. As the pocket calculator has atrophied the ability to perform mental arithmetic, so the computer takes away **PERSONAL SKILL** and may deaden creativity, if it is not wisely used. For the maker who is interested in an **INTEGRATED EXPERIENCE** the computer will be useful. At the same time, anything that separates the maker from the direct experience that once guided the work may be harmful in the long term. Making is a highly physical experience, so any technique that removes the maker from contact with the material

Paradigm: A pattern of thinking based on experience. A paradigm is a quick way to consider the range of possibilities. Paradigms can contain our thinking, but when we search for a paradigm shift or a new paradigm, we are open to possibilities.

Those who believe they can do
something and those who believe
they can't, both are right.

HENRY FORD

and the procedures of production and problem solving will interfere with his or her ability to create a work of substance. Engineering, architecture, and industrial design all tend to suffer in this way. Even when a computer is used daily and intensively, there is still the need to roll up one's sleeves and spend time at the workbench.

TRANSFORMATION best describes what happens when the visual experience is used imaginatively. The transformation takes place not only in the subject and object, but also in the person creating the subject and object. The object is the evidence of the maker's new insight into the subject. The transformation of a child to an adult, or a novice creator to a fully developed artist, is complex. Some of it seems to happen automatically, some takes a good deal of trial and error, and some develops after careful interrogation of the problem. Not all ideas solve problems. The engineer may solve the

problem by taking us from one side of the river to the other in the most efficient physical manner. Another person may choose to express the inner reality of his or her experience of the other side of the river. The drawing of the other side of the river may be tranquil and optimistic, or mysterious and foreboding—either way, we are taken across the river to different personal realities. Our job or our emotional experience both can influence the way we tackle the work and the transformation of crossing.

The activity of creation requires different strategies and practices, which depend on expectations. Does the object have an intended purpose, or does the expectation lie in the pleasure of the creative process? Creativity has to be considered from the viewpoint of who is creating, what mental and emotional processes are they using, and what are their environmental and cultural influences?

New Grange II
1993

Embroidered hand-made paper and
fabric, printing blocks and inks
12 cm dia x 6 cm
Mary Crehan
Woodbridge, Suffolk, UK

Mary Crehan is an Irish person living in Woodbridge and her influences are from Neolithic Passage tombs in Ireland. Crehan embroiders paper and fabric to make earthbound objects that resonate with earlier cultures. It is through the combining and recombining of materials and technologies that new forms and a sense of the original are created. Ancient forms and materials can engage the viewer at an instinctual level; as Crehan points out, *"A significant shape has always been that of the bowl. Making bowls of various sizes I used them to carry the designs, symbols and markings of Neolithic Man. Currently I am working on a large shallow vessel known archaeologically as a 'Basin Stone,' and a wall hanging based on 'Orthostat 54.' These are expressions of the Great Basin Stone and Orthostat found in the tomb at Knowth."*

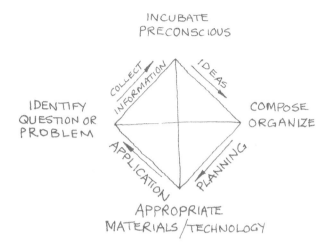

When creativity is placed in the context of the four disciplines of art, craft/technology, design, and science, the processes tend to differentiate. Art tends to be **PERCEPTUAL**, craft is **MOTOR/PHYSICAL**, design is **ORGANIZATIONAL** and science is **COGNITIVE**. One aspect that does seem to be common to all disciplines is the **NEED TO ITERATE**, that is, the need to do it again—to iterate and reiterate. The most familiar pattern may be represented by the diagram.

It is possible to start at any of the major points; however, most often people proceed as follows:

▷ Identify a **QUESTION** to answer, a **PROBLEM** to investigate or an **ISSUE** to solve. Research associated and relevant information.

▷ Before ideas can be properly realized there is an **INCUBATION TIME** when patience is rewarded by the preconscious, which presents solutions. These ideas must be evaluated in relationship to the question, problem, or issue.

▷ The ideas take on a visual appearance, which may be organized around composition or context. The **ORGANIZATION** leads to **PLANNING** for production.

▷ What **METHODS OF MAKING** will be used?

▷ What is the appropriate technology?

▷ Having made the idea, it is applied to the situation for which it was intended. **ACTION** has been taken.

Some creativity emphasizes the body: it is concerned with materials and physicality. Other creativity emphasizes the mind: it is concerned with ideas and knowledge. Both are equally important in a well rounded person and in an egalitarian society.

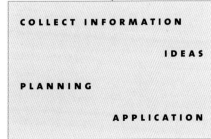

COLLECT INFORMATION

IDEAS

PLANNING

APPLICATION

> "One can't believe impossible things."
> "I daresay you haven't had much practice,"
> said the Queen. "When I was your age, I always
> did it for half-an-hour a day. Why, sometimes
> I've believed as many as six impossible
> things before breakfast."
>
> LEWIS CARROLL
> THROUGH THE LOOKING-GLASS

PRECONSCIOUS CREATIVITY

It is possible to make a game of creativity—perhaps all creativity has a foundation in play—but more important than play is openness and flexibility. What if, why not, let's try? In a more profound sense, play helps us act out our dreams, desires, and aspirations; play leads us to SELF-REALIZATION where we become our potentialities. Any creative person will attest to the "OH WOW" of what has been discovered and realized. This sense of wonderment is essential to the creative experience.

The things that are made in the creative process act as TRANSITIONAL OBJECTS between ourselves and others. Mixed into the activity of play is the range of emotions such as fear, desire, and aggression, as well as the more altruistic concerns of generosity, caring, and giving. The unconscious motivations that inspire the consciousness to action are complex. The artist will usually be influenced by, or will work directly with, the HUMAN IMPULSE from the unconscious that represents his or her experience in the work. This does not make the work unthinking but it does make space for other dimensions beyond the strictly average, objective, and rational.

DREAMS, RANDOM IMAGES, and JUXTAPOSITION OF UNEXPECTED ELEMENTS are the basis of SURREALISM and other styles of 20th century art. By placing two images together, it is possible to change their context and create a new and bewildering or surprising experience. The painter Rene Magritte placed a rock and a cloud in the sky, both of an equivalent size. Forms and materials placed in unfamiliar relationships can have the same effect. Meret Openheim's teacup lined with fur is disorienting—its tactile quality confronts the expectation of a refreshing liquid. This is a form of creativity that takes place in a contemplative manner and is difficult to force, control, or predict—which is a large part of its attraction. The fascination is with the unknown and unexpected. The projects are often paradoxical. Rational and linear thinking gives way to a lateral, pattern-seeking approach. Within this approach the artist mediates between a situation and the viewer. What is presented is not an explanation, rather it is an image or environment that enables viewers to think more deeply and profoundly about the subject and their response to it.

PHYSICAL CREATIVITY

An important part of play is response to and creation with physical materials, whether they come from the environment, or from the scientist in the laboratory. In the environment there are three STATES OF MATTER of which everything is composed: gases, liquids, and solids. Matter has PHYSICAL PROPERTIES of mass, odor, color, texture, and luster. Although these are the essentials of matter as defined by science, our experience of the mix of these elements is wonderfully complex.

The variations of visual contrasts and elements attract us first, then we perceive such properties as weight, temperature, hardness, smoothness, softness, rough tactility, sharpness or prickliness. Qualities of skin, fur, hair, porcupine quills or fish scales become apparent. Part of creative play is the allure of working with such qualities as the sensuality of one material, the repulsive consistency of another, or the implied meaning of another. By placing one material next to another in sharp contrasts or subtle blends, it is possible to evoke emotions. Sometimes the artist reinvents

the qualities found in nature and presents new possibilities.

When created materials are placed in the context of designed objects and environments, it is possible to see how the maker was motivated to express MEANING THROUGH MATERIALS. The meaning is guided by desire for the juxtaposition of wonderfully colored and textured materials. A quite satisfactory relationship. Carried too far it becomes reminiscent of the riches from the past. The association with imperial power may unfortunately become an additional stimulation for some ideologically disempowered people. Displays of wealth through materials is still concerned with power relations and can move the object beyond physical creativity.

When one works with materials and ignores CONTEXT, there is one less layer of meaning. But it is not possible to create a thing and not find it in a context of some sort. The context may offer a function or purpose against which the juxtaposition of materials and skill can be evaluated. Much of creativity comes from an appreciation of materials, how they are worked, how they fit together, their strength and durability, environmental impact, and appropriateness to circumstance.

> I love the mystery that can happen with slowness.
> You can't do anything good quickly.
> Waiting and watching are keys.
>
> ✎
> MICHAEL LEVINE

Super Bowl: Energy free waterer, Model 4 x 4
1987

36 x 38 x 17"
Rotationally molded plastic
and concrete pad
SPi
Bruce County, Ontario, Canada

Appearance of this product is simple. Livestock put their nose in and take a drink. But its simplicity is deceptive: through the ingenuity of insulation and detailing, the simple box saves enormous amounts of energy, the farmer's time, and the livestock's health. An energy-free waterer was first used by the Mennonites of rural Pennsylvania. It solved the problem of farm animals getting water in freezing conditions, without the regular intervention of the farmer or the use of electricity. Stray voltage does have a way of putting the animals "off their water" and , at worst, do them in completely. Ground water has a regular temperature regardless of location so the problem was to maintain that temperature for as long as possible in the waterer. SPi of Shallow Lake worked with the basic concept and designed a super-insulated model that could withstand the rigors of Northern Canada and sub-zero temperatures. Since the first tests in 1986 many new problems have been solved and patents applied for. At approximately a dollar a day for a conventional heated waterer, massive savings were to be made for farmers in cold climates. Super Bowl also works in warm climates. Algae-free water, and less chance of heat stress for livestock, have taken this ingenious solution to over 20 different countries.

Certain materials carry cultural significance through the MYTHS AND BELIEF SYSTEMS of their culture. It is important for the maker to understand what the significant blends are, and how these juxtapositions arose. That the jewelry is made from gold is for some people infinitely more important than its form or concept. The value of materials is also noticeable in architecture. The materials of the factory are usually the cheapest, as compared to public buildings (especially in the past) where the finest materials and workmanship were employed. Today the pretense or illusion of quality more often than not is what counts in public. Corporate architecture and private homes are where the physical is most highly regarded. The carefully constructed public realm, the democratically shared space, is resented because it represents too much tax dollars at work. At the extreme this view leads to a mean and narrow view of our collective selves.

PROBLEM SOLVING

A need arises that requires a solution. This is often referred to as the PROBLEM. Not all of life is a problem. Sometimes it is simply searching for a PURPOSE. For example, a collector needs to store objects recently acquired. They could be stored in the basement or attic but the purpose is really to see the collection at will. The designer analyzes all the needs, synthesizes a solution, and knows what to do. To find the solution the designer will follow specific strategies for unraveling the possible routes to be taken. The process in its simplest form is to analyze, then synthesize.

ANALYZE—SYNTHESIZE

First it is necessary to gather the facts and sort out what it is we are trying to solve. In the example of the collector, "all the facts" includes the possibility of rearranging a room. The designer sees the possibility of a relationship between the storage and display of the collection, and the arrangement of rooms. Working in a linear pattern, the problem is studied, ideas are sorted, and a solution is selected.

PURPOSE—IDEAS—SOLUTION

This is the basis of most creative problem solving. It is difficult to direct creativity without knowing what is to be solved. To evaluate an idea, it is necessary to have succinctly defined the need. By defining the need there is a criterion for evaluation, feedback from beginning to end. The simple form of problem—idea—solution expands from a linear process to include a definition of the needs to be solved and a careful evaluation of the solution based on the definition. The problem is redefined to include permanent display and storage in a manner that allows easy access and security while maximizing viewing. The problem has been changed to a new purpose—it becomes proactive and positive. Forget the basement!

FACTS—DEFINITION—IDEAS— SOLUTION—EVALUATION

The pattern of the activity not only moves forward, but also circles back in different sized loops that finally encompass the whole activity. What are the facts, all the facts, at this point? The room is redesigned, new furniture can be added, the purpose of the room can be adapted and a partition wall can be removed. It is decided to store the collection in a transparent wall that divides the space into two rooms. Storage was the issue but by redefining the perceived problem and redefining the issue with all the facts it became possible to have ideas and develop solutions that incidentally became easier to evaluate. Final evaluation and selection is simplified when the subject has been researched, there is a clear definition of what must be solved, and there are many choices to evaluate. The best solution often stands out as the right way to go and action can be taken with some confidence.

FACTS—DEFINITION—IDEAS— SOLUTION—EVALUATION— ACTION

SCIENTIFIC METHOD

The SCIENTIFIC METHOD involves asking questions and PROPOSING HYPOTHESES to develop knowledge. Knowing the right question to ask can be the key to an appropriate investigation and desired conclusion. The question may be a supposition, which will become the basis for reasoning. An assumption or series of observations generates a hypothesis, which becomes the starting point: What happens when two colors are mixed together? They will become another color, and we can proceed to investigate and experiment to find out if that is true and if so, what the third color will be under different conditions. David Pye wrote, "Invention is the process of discovering a principle. Design is the process of applying that principle." Problem solving is usually about APPLYING PRINCIPLES, whereas the scientific method is concerned with ESTABLISHING PRINCIPLES. To discover a new principle it is necessary to carry out experiments that will verify or disprove the imagined hypothesis.

Any EXPERIMENT should be set up in a simple and, if possible, elegant manner. The experimenter is looking for the most effect from the least affect. In an elegant process it is easier to observe the subtleties, and perhaps to see possibilities that might not occur or might be masked in a clumsy process. The procedure for an experiment would include:

PURPOSE—INFORMATION—HYPOTHESIS—
EXPERIMENT—PROCEDURE—OBSERVATION—
CONCLUSION

Many great inventions come from an INTUITIVE LEAP, albeit one that is well founded in a through knowledge of the subject. In complex projects like the design of a snowmobile for Arctic use, one needs more than just an intuitive leap or hunch that this idea will work. Rather, one needs a process that interrogates all aspects of the problem and leaves nothing to chance, because chance may well leave the operator in serious trouble in the severe conditions of the far North. The beauty and subtlety of the intuitive leap must be followed by examination, careful experiment, and observation.

> Whatever we have been given is supposed to be given away again, not kept... The only essential is this: the gift must always move.
>
> ∽
> LEWIS HYDE
> THE GIFT

PAYING ATTENTION

Collect all the facts about the situation—research the topic. Notice what does not fit. The anomaly may offer useful insight and present new possibilities. Allow the inquiry to guide you toward a truth.

CONCLUSION

Each of the four methods has a relationship to the others. The emphasis of the person creating the approach become evident through the results. It is impossible to be exclusively one thing or to take a watertight position. The seepage is always evident, if you know how to look critically at situations. That is the job of the critic, to evaluate creative contributions to the society. Criticism is examined in depth in Chapter 10.

In all creative processes it is necessary to exercise imagination, to see the situation in a new way and try to make improvements that are ethical. Is it original? Do the ideas behind the work return to the origins? New ideas at their best always return us to our origins. Throughout the text questions of appropriateness are discussed but it is in religion and philosophy that these issues are dealt with in detail.

By themselves computers do not solve problems but they do help with complexity. They can facilitate creative solutions to information-related problems. However, it is often quicker and possibly better to pick up a pencil and do the drawing, make the calculation on the back of an envelope, or write the letter by hand. The material relationship of mind-brain-hand needs regular attention if a person is to remain fully operational and creative.

Grace: Homage to Earth and Sky for Food and Water
1995

Mixed Media Installation
House: 96 x 52 x 73"
Table: 90 x 70" dia
Kathleen Edwards
Woodacre, California, USA

Grace: Homage to Earth and Sky for Food and Water shows the shrine-like entrance to a larger installation. Beyond the entrance a table is set with food and utensils and four chairs. The table and chairs are highly imaginary and fantastic, yet rooted in the familiar. In contrast the entrance is a small vestibule lined with canned food from supermarkets and rainwater collected in recycled glass jars. Janice Sandeen makes reference to how "the table and settings are made from different kinds of earth and fibers from edible plants such as fennel (table and chairs), corn husks (mats), and walnuts (spoons). Kathleen Edwards coordinated the donation from local supermarkets of all the food used in the house piece, and then donated the food at the close of the installation to the Marin Community Food Bank." The work is a stunning reminder that every day we transform the environment through our bodies to stay alive. Grace: Homage to Earth and Sky for Food and Water points out the importance of process and of the sensory, critical, and mental transformations we make in the wonderful mystery of life.

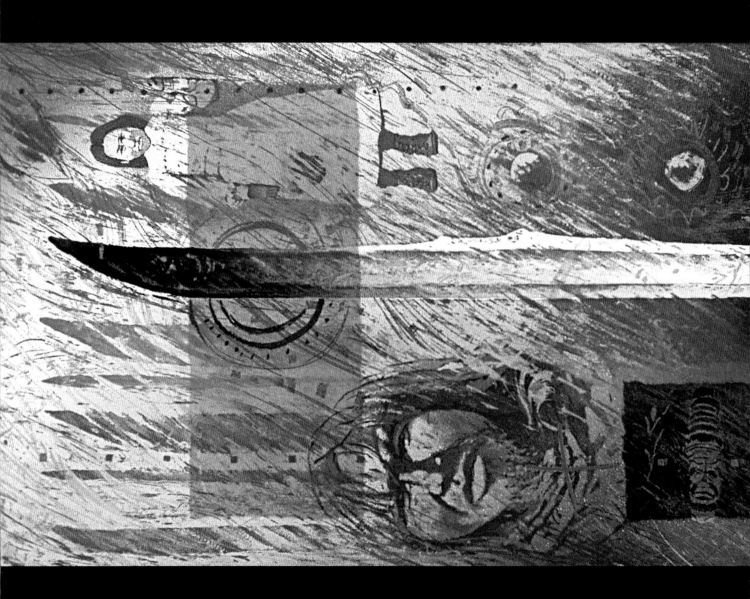

Silent Boats

The kayak is, for Allen Smutylo, a means of transportation in the far north of Canada. It offers access to some dramatic and awesome

becomes harmonized, which offers complete focus on the subject. For Smutylo, the painter, landscape, and inhabitants become his source of

shows the Inuit Kayak at rest. The elegant fragile form is waiting for the spring break-up of thick ice. Having traveled and recorded like the

CHAPTER SIX

Self and Other

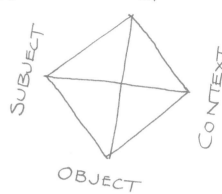

OVERVIEW

Concepts relating to Self and Other expand to include object and context. The binary split is replaced by four relationships. This makes an appreciation for Self and Other less complex. The four areas are seen in relationship to perceptual and conceptual ways of experiencing and thinking about appearance.

DIVERSITY

In each discipline there are different perspectives from which to analyze SELF, OBJECT, SUBJECT, and CONTEXT. Ultimately some work will seem right in every way, and it will sometimes be referred to as a UNIVERSAL SOLUTION or a TIMELESS OBJECT. What this really means is that a society was able to reach a point of consensus (or forced the idea on the public) at a given moment: the work rings true for many people. Today we have moved beyond Modernism's preoccupation with one universal solution. There is a greater appreciation for difference, which also results in a high degree of fragmentation. Some of this fragmentation has opened up possibilities for diverse groups of people who might otherwise have been excluded. In this new form of modernity, the challenge is to maintain openness without total anarchy.

    The relation of Self to Other is the basis of the analysis of the four areas of self, subject, object, and context. Often these four points of interest will get

SELF

CONTEXT

OBJECT

SUBJECT

split apart or placed in a hierarchy, which creates misconceptions and friction. In this section the relationship between these four points, how they interact, and why they need one another will be explored. The Self must remain critically aware of the relationships among self, subject, object, and context.

> Don't shoot. I am a
> British Object
> ↩
> FROM REMEMBERING BABYLON

SELF

Each person has his or her own particular and unique way of perceiving the world. We each have to develop our own relationship to the external experience. There is an activity inside the person/self that is as important as the activity outside the person/self. The self will think about a subject and the subject will become part of that person's experience: the self and the subject become one. Some people will make an object that relates to an experience in part to understand the experience and in part to proclaim or record their understanding of the experience. To do it, make it, or experience it will cement the mental concept into an external reality—an object.

The self is sometimes called the only subject. The painter or photographer makes or takes a self-portrait: the subject is the self. They may also create images of the land and perhaps the land is in turmoil. The turmoil may be an expression of the artist's or photographer's experience. He or she is drawn to the image of turmoil because s/he identifies with it or empathizes with the condition. It graphically portrays experience. The swirling brush strokes in his landscapes portrays the turmoil of Vincent van Gogh's life—the subject of the land and the artist's self are unified. More often, self and subject are not unified in such a clear and dramatic manner. The subject is objectified by the rational, conscious side of the mind.

It is important to realize that a stormy image does not necessarily express the maker's inner experience. The creator of the image may be demonstrating or illustrating an idea outside his or her personal experience for reasons of gain rather than of expression. For example, advertising often employs images of sexuality and wealth because this is the easiest way to create desire in the viewer. The image of a storm juxtaposed with a brightly colored, well lighted house will suggest the home as a nurturing and protective environment. Conversely, the derelict house may suggest a personally stormy interior experience.

The self is strongly influenced by many factors that direct the comprehension and representation of subject. AGE, GENDER, ORIENTATION, RACE, and RELIGION are a few of the lenses through which the self will experience and then create work that is particular to the individual in society. A chair may take a particular form because of a person's age— either very young or old. A nursing mother will have definite preferences for a particular chair that is not too deep, squishy, or low. The arms of the chair must aid relaxed holding of the child(ren). Some chairs appeal to the masculine side rather than the feminine side of a personality. Big and bold compared to slight and elegant suggests different ways of sitting that may be appropriate for either a man or a woman. People in some cultures sit lower to the ground than others do. In the past, a chair with arms at the dining table indicated authority and usually was placed at the "head" of the table. The iconography carved into furniture may represent the belief system of a religious group. Modern industrial chairs usually deny these expressions and are designed for the average secular person but that too, while not religious, has ideological implications.

The subject animates the object. The person is a living being, not only because he or she has a material form, but also because he or she is a thinking, feeling entity. Each person has consciousness—an ego that is their subjective side, where the moral side of behavior is formed. The object, or person, has a subject, a conscious self.

SUBJECT

Looking at art or at a line of books on a shelf, we are not only looking at objects but also are considering subjects: each work of art and each book has its own subject. This relationship can reverse when the subject of the book is objects. These object-subject relationships are what is of interest. Each discipline tends to emphasize either the OBJECTIVE and CONCRETE, or the SUBJECTIVE and IMMATERIAL, but within a discipline you will find both approaches. A building or a bridge may be highly objective and functional, using materials in a mean and hard manner with little apparent feeling for the people

Miss Sailing Arrives for Sunday School
1995

Acrylic on canvas board
900 x 600 cm
Leann Edwards
Lakes Entrance, Victoria, Australia

Leann Edwards paints in a naive manner—perspective, proportion, scale, subject matter, and human relations are all distorted for the story. With whom do we identify in the image? The central image is the woman in the turquoise dress. A group of children in the foreground hides behind the tall grass—the viewer is

physically closest to the group —while other children peer from behind the buildings. The viewer is seen and the central figure looks out at us and waves. We are invited to take a stand on Miss Sailing's Sunday School.

The political and religious underpinnings are devastating in the context of

the aboriginal experience as manipulated by Eurocentric myths of church and god. Do we help Miss Sailing push the children into the clearing to join the Sunday school, or do we stand back and denounce what has been done? The naiveté of the painting works like an apology in the interplay among self, subject, object, and context.

Rosie Baldwin 751 Kearny St. Port Townsend USA 76308

Laird's Landing Letters:
Water Conservation
1984

Envelope, stamp, ink, water colors
6 x 4"
Clayton Lewis
California, USA

Clayton Lewis was, throughout his life, interested and active in many disciplines. Between 1980 and 1987 he created approximately 500 pieces of envelope art. The envelope acts as a direct reference to communication between people. The Water Conservation image shows two people in conversation, looking out at the viewer. The two people probably are the same person—two sides or two selves of being human, the restrained self on the left and the over-indulged self on the right. The skull at their feet confirms the reading. Lewis often works this kind of device into his envelope art, making no bones about the codes that guide our behavior. Cartooning often is a skillful manipulation of self, subject, context, and object; Lewis was a story teller and this can be seen in his envelope art. He told the following story which, although not directly connected to this image, reveals a profound relationship:

"Breakfast by the bay on my beautiful, wild beach is one recurring pleasure for me. I witness the continuous ferment at the edge of things—where the water meets the land. This morning the new sun grandly illuminates everything— apparent contradictions and all. An eternal beginning."
Clayton Lewis, July 30, 1980

using the structure. The painter may use his imagination to the point of creating a nonsense of subject that has no basis in reality and adds nothing to the way we see ourselves. However, through the imagination a painter may also present the fantastic and paradoxical as a metaphor for everyday experience—and the massive bridge may have all the grace of a fine line in tension.

When object and subject are working well together, we find the material presence of object along with the apprehension of meaning in subject. The architecture of the Museum of Civilisation in Ottawa, by Douglas Cardinal, is a particularly strong example of the coming together of the objective (computer aided) design and the subjective feelings of the architect. The landscaping, walls, and windows are made from long, graceful and complex curves. The forms evoke the land, the river at the site, and the gentle spirit of the wind in summer.

> My work is not made for Indian people but for thinking people. In the global and evolutionary scheme, the difference between humans is negligible.
>
> CARL BEAM

OBJECT

An object is a solid point, line, or form—it is either a material thing or a depiction of one. The object may be a computer, a tree, the neighbor's dog, or another person. The object can also be what we direct our feelings toward. It can be a one-way experience, in which case we OBJECTIFY what we look at. There is no EMPATHY. We look at the object without thoughts and feelings for our RELATIONSHIP to the object and its subject. ICONS are objects. The icon objectifies the subject. The subject may be about anything, though (non-computer) icons often are associated with religion. The image, statue, or mosaic can be sacred, a thing of worship. Today people make icons of worship and desire of their cars, televisions, boats. Their belief structure is entwined with the meanings of the object and how they are seen objectified by others. By assembling objects around themselves, people create a context for meaning. The subject or idea gets lost in an emotional clutch of how the objects project their image. But these are extreme pathological examples from societies of abundance, and tend to be less problematic in cultures that live closer to the land.

An ICONOGRAPHER studies the subject matter of art. Iconography is the subject of the object and it is in the subject that meaning may be constructed or sought. The subjective side is where the moral aspect of behavior is formed. The problems start when people believe what they are told through the icon, rather than having a relationship to the subject through the iconography.

SUBJECT-OBJECT RELATIONS, and the balance of one with the other, have been central to the maker's experience. SUBJECT and CONTENT or OBJECT and FORM have always pulled back and forth for the maker. What is more important, the idea of the project, or the form of the project? If I get the form right it will look after the idea. If I look after the idea the form will evolve as it should. Mies van der Rohe said that "god is in the details." This is yet another bias of one thing over another, though one that can also be understood as the details of subject and object. The problems start when there is too much specialization in either object or subject. Including self and context helps break the binary deadlock and its oppositional response, creating a more balanced view.

CONTEXT

The separation or oppositional confrontation of object and subject can be reduced by always taking context into account. Object and subject must have a context. It is as necessary as the space around the form: you cannot see the form without seeing the space surrounding it. The quality of light on an object can change what we feel about it; the object can shift from being mild and innocent to being threatening and terrifying.

JUXTAPOSITION and RELATION of an object will change from one context to another. The swastika is a dramatic example. Before the Nazis it was a benign symbol for the sun, but it became a horrible symbol after the holocaust of World War Two.

Advertising deliberately uses context to persuade the viewer of the importance of products. Soft drinks are not much more than flavored water but the context of happy, young, beautiful, and wealthy people convinces consumers to buy millions of cans each day.

Every artist, craftsperson, designer, or scientist has to consider the context of their object and subject. The scientist Frank Oppenheimer and his team worked during World War Two on nuclear fission and the atomic bomb. The context seemed to justify the ends. Now we have the new context of nuclear waste from power stations and weapons production. It does rather dramatically present a context on the edge of insanity. For the maker of simple objects like tool handles, the context of use has to be thought about. How will the handle work for people of different ages, gender, and disabilities? Perhaps this is an issue of design and form rather than of making, but ultimately more than one discipline will overlap. The painter Rene Magritte wittily, provocatively, and insightfully represented

A student of James Whistler claimed to paint what he saw. Whistler replied, "But the shock will come when you see what you paint."

Mage
1983

Redwood
96 x 51 x 27"
J.B. Blunk
Inverness, California, USA

Mage is slightly taller than the viewer but we relate to the sculpture as equivalent to ourselves. It is both raw and cooked and carries an emotional quality. Controlled and smooth in the lower area while bursting forth in wildly fluid gesture, yet it remains poised, dramatically frozen in space. How easy it is to relate to the emotional impulse that bursts forth with exuberant energy. The form, coaxed from what was a living tree, is inverted. Roots that searched for water in the ground now search the sky.

Mage is an archaic term for magician, learned person. Perhaps it is a metaphor that is open in its meanings for what the viewer will see and feel. Do we see ourselves as uprooted, turned around and free to express ourselves, or do we see the redwood tree afresh as another form which, to survive, must put down these extraordinary roots? The mystery of life and the magic of sculpture brings the viewer closer to the Other.

subjects and objects out of context. A rock floating in the sky or a carrot metamorphosing into a wine bottle playfully reconstructs objects, suggesting a new context and ambiguous meaning.

The **PERCEPTUAL** and **CONCEPTUAL** are two ways to experience appearance. The perceptual is based in the physiology of how the eye and brain work to see appearance. The conceptual is what the mind thinks about seeing in a symbolic shorthand. When analyzing an object, image, or environment perceptually, it is important to work through both the objective and subjective aspects, and to see how they are contextualized. By drawing an object a perceptual intimacy can be developed, which the casual glance will deny. By drawing the shape, surface quality, shadows and highlights, the physical form can be appreciated in great depth. There is an angle from which most objects are represented; drawing a familiar form from an unexpected angle will demand more attention. Careful observation may reveal the marks of production processes, the flaws of chipped paint, and traces of the object's own story.

Making the form in other materials will offer contrasting surfaces. Claes Oldenburg made familiar objects like *Hamburger, Soft Toilet* and *Soft Giant Drum Set* from materials not normally associated with those objects. This perceptual twisting of the senses leads the viewer to construct a new conceptual attitude toward that type of object. Changing the scale helps the maker or viewer to see the form in a new way. This will be a perceptual way of thinking and feeling about the object.

The conceptual way of thinking and feeling about the object would be to modify some aspect of the form or color to surprise the way we normally think about it. We thought we understood this form, but it appears to have another subject than the one we normally associate with it. When two objects are brought together and are hybridized, they create a third and unexpected combination. Conversely, two subjects may be brought together into a single object. Jana Sterbak has made a work in the form of a dress that is made from steaks which rot away on exhibition. In another of her installations, titled *I Want You to Feel the Way I Do... (The Dress)*, the dress is made from live uninsulated nickel-chrome wire mesh. Behind this is a projected text that starts out *I want you to feel the way I do: ...* While perceptually we relate and respond to the work with a physical response, we soon engage with it on a conceptual level. The Minimalists attempted to reduce the physical and perceptual aspect to pure idea, but the best works consider both the mind and body placed in context.

The context for some work can be quite specific. Maya Lin's Vietnam War Memorial in Washington is a fine and moving example where self, subject,

Craftsmanship
1995

Digital imaging for a
woodworking brochure
Frances Evelegh
Newmarket, Suffolk, UK

Frances Evelegh works with
computers and digital imaging.
In this image for a woodworking
brochure the elements draw us
into the subject of blunt saws.
The clock establishes context, 5:30
is quitting time for many people.
The blades are the objects of our
concern: new blades mean safer,
faster, more accurate work. Yellow
is often used as a cautionary color;
the bent-over figure burns red-hot
from the frustration of changing
blunt blades. The image
encourages caution, the purchase
and replacement of new saw
blades. What is interesting in the
image is how the designer
sublimates Self to seduce the
Other. We do not know the
designer any better, however
much we relate to and admire
the image. Such is life for the
advertising designer.

object, and context connect in a unified experience. The work is
eminently approachable and understandable, yet it presents the great
mystery of life and death. Richard Long's installation work is absolutely in
the context of where he finds the materials. He would travel thousands
of miles to a specific place in order to present a line or circle of rocks or
branches in the environment in which they were found. He would
photograph the work, then leave it as part of the landscapes much like
a cairn or Inuit marker.

The gallery has isolated the work from context but today there are
many artists who first work with context and process, then with subject
and object. Another way of thinking about an object in a gallery would
be to see it as an isolated form withdrawn from its usual context.
Now that it is isolated, its power and presence may be reduced—or
perhaps increased.

Know all Men by these Presents:

That *Mr A. G. Weeks* and *C. S. Weeks husband*
and wife

of *Caldwell* County, State of ___, in consideration of the sum of

Four ___ DOLLARS,

in hand paid by *Joseph Betts*

Guthrie County, State of *Iowa*

hereby acknowledge, have bargained ___

___ *Joseph Betts*

and to the following described premises:

Lots Nine (9) and ___ *in Block Eight*
in the Original Town ___
Iowa

With ___ the hereditaments ___ appurtenances thereto belonging.

Signed this *29th* day of ___ ___ A. D. 1882

SIGNED IN PRESENCE OF

B. McDilley

A. G. Weeks
C. S. Weeks

STATE OF *Missouri*
Caldwell County.

I, *B. McDilley*

___ Notary Public

in ___ for said County, do hereby ___

G. Weeks and C. S. ___ before ___ this day personally came

personally known to be the ___ ___ husband wife

___ deed, as grantors, and ack ___ ___ whose ___ ___ affixed to the

___ to be ___ voluntary act ___ the said instrument, and the execution

___ this *29th* ___ ___ ___ January ___ 83

April A. D. 1882

B. McDilley, Notary Public

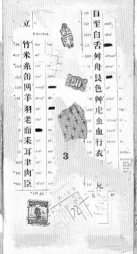

立 竹米糸舌岡羊羽老而耒耳聿肉臣

目至白舌舛舟艮色艸虍虫血行衣

兄

No. 708

STATE OF ___
OFFICE OF COUNTY AUDITOR,
GUTHRIE COUNTY, SS.

Montana

B. Tindell

Auditor's Certificate,

TOTAL,

Presented to and Cancelled this ___
day of *Sept* 1883 ___ *Foster*

$65

46   NEW FIRST READER.

LESSON XXXVII.

peach   ly-ing
beach   nice ___
reach   largo   fry-ing
teach   what   try-ing

O Ma-ry, do come and see the peach!
Is it not a nice large one?
Is the peach for me, or is it for you?

boy   milk   bread
what   but-ter
said   gives   din-
your   which   dri-

An old man met a boy ___ a cow.
The old man said, My lad, what is you
cow ___ for?
The boy said, Our cow gives milk.
From milk we make but-ter. We
but-ter with bread for our din-ter

Communication

Opened by Censor
1992

Mixed media—collage
& acrylic on paper
23 x 30"
Kit Artig
Bolinas, California, USA

Opened by Censor is a shocking idea that seems harmless enough when you stand well back from the details in the work. The design of the image is seductive and gentle; it floats in a firm composition. The desecration by the censor is somewhere else— in the details—where the censor is often to be found. On closer inspection of the collaged image some words are deleted, interrupting the flow of messages. I search from one scrap of paper to another looking for consistency in the deletions, but it is arbitrary. The deletions seem irrelevant in the puzzle of what is lost to the viewer and they create a response of "how dare they control the message."

The deletions are mixed up with images of imperialism, officialdom, and authority, which code the representation as them-against-us. At the top of the image are the words "Know all men by these presents." Presents can be pronounced with an emphasis on the second "e," to present a show and tell, or to give away a present. In this context, "presents" means charge or indictment What a complex word re-present-ation becomes!

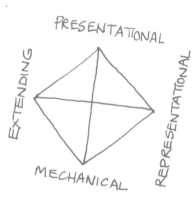

OVERVIEW

There is a close relationship between the how and what of any visual appearance—communication is one consequence of IMAGE-MAKING. Communication is concerned with how appearance is transmitted by the maker and received by the viewer. Image-making is concerned with what and who gets represented. The diagram shows four ways to present and communicate something. These four modes can all be observed within the contexts of art, craft/technology, design, and science.

COMMUNICATION

SIGNS AND CODES are fundamental to communication. Signs are ACTS and ARTIF-ACTS that refer to something other than themselves. A sign may be part of a group of signs that forms a code. The code is a system that helps determine how one sign relates to another. A traffic stop-sign is part of a system of traffic signals that together form a code. Morse code is a system of dots and dashes that spells out signs representing individual letters, which themselves are the signs of the alphabet. The 1-and-o digital code of the computer is yet another code with broad implications for our culture, but also with its own limitations.

PRESENTATIONAL

REPRESENTATIONAL

MECHANICAL

EXTENSIONAL

Township
1992

Acrylic on paper
210 x 210 cm
William Young
Morwell, Victoria, Australia

The painting is predominantly red and brown—the colors of the earth—except for an unexpected purple-blue hue cast through a light such as the setting sun. Central in the image is a patch of green. A green space is next to the house and on the opposite side from the quarry. On the green patch a regular scale shovel rests in sharp contrast to the tiny house. The handle projects out above a community of miniature houses, across the edge of a box. The box is made from a distorted flimsy cardboard construction and set on a table. At the tip of the shovel's blade there is a cut-out element. The cut-out has an archway and what might be spaces for windows or the spaces between columns on a building. There is a sense of a model being transported from one place to another, or of elements from several projects thrown into a casual or unexpected juxtaposition in the cardboard box.

All the parts in the painting are signifiers coded towards a particular idea. The artist has displayed the objects out of their familiar context so that we might see them in a new play. The box suggests production with the handle of the shovel inviting us to pick it up and dig in. The only area left to dig is the green patch. The quarry or strip mine is as deep as the shovel blade; the community cannot be dug without destroying the homes. Who will destroy the remaining green space?

The shadows suggest several light sources even though the feeling of a setting sun pervades the work. A dark shadow casts across the tiny settlement. Familiar objects code the painting to present ideas of work and environment. The light source codes the mood and fills the image with the end of a day's work, or (more likely) the end to the relentless use and misuse of the environment. The painting is coded with images of work, homes, the facade of institutions, and the collective problems of the actual cardboard model in which we work and play. The model signifies a theoretical projection of a system in trouble and about to be remodeled or discarded.

114

There are two main schools of thinking about communications: the **PROCESS SCHOOL**, which involves the transmission of messages, and the **SEMIOTIC SCHOOL**, which involves the production and exchange of meanings. The process school is more concerned with **RESTRICTED CODES** because they are more descriptive, easier to understand, and they tend to keep society together. The semiotic school is more concerned with **ELABORATED CODES**, which are more analytic and concerned with complexities within the specific code. Restricted codes and elaborated codes perform different functions.

Road signs are an example of a restricted code. Codes like these are used daily, and society generally understands and collectively agrees on their meaning. The elaborated code is analytic and more complex. It investigates the complexity of relationships within the code. Some science writing is an example of an elaborated code that communicates only among specialists in the same field. Scientists in other fields may be unable to follow it. Similarly, some contemporary art practice also communicates only to the specialist. Not all art results in an easily recognizable image. The Uniform Building Code is an example from the craft/technology sector that falls midway between restricted code and elaborated code.

All codes rely on commonality and agreement. If nobody understands it, then it communicates nothing. Agreement is reached in three fundamental ways: by convention and use, for example road signs; by explicit agreement, for example building codes, which nevertheless may need interpretation by a specialist; and by clues in the text, for example, scientific essays.

MODES OF COMMUNICATION

There are four main modes for communication.

PRESENTATIONAL MEDIA: voice, face, body, and the presence of the communicator.

REPRESENTATIONAL MEDIA: paintings, writing, sculpture, craft, graphics, architecture, Internet, and the works of the communicator.

MECHANICAL MEDIA: books, telephone, radio, films and video, and the Internet are transmitters of both presentational and representational media. These mechanical media are converging and can be intermixed when they are based on the common signs used in digital processing and communications.

EXTENSIONAL MEDIA: electron microscope, X ray photography, radio telescope and any means that reaches beyond the unaugmented sensorium.

When a message is communicated through any material, technology, or media, it may be familiar, predictable, and conventional—and consequently low in information. Advertising will often have these characteristics, especially in a crowded environment. Other communications may be low in predictability but with the potential of being high in information. Trade journals and specialist articles with their attendant advertisements often present new, unfamiliar, and unconventional information. New art forms, new technology, and new science are all difficult to read precisely because they are new—they do not fit established patterns in the mind. This may lead to immediate rejection, to caution, or to study of the new ideas in order to evaluate and integrate them into personal experience. Information that is simple to comprehend is audience-centered and about

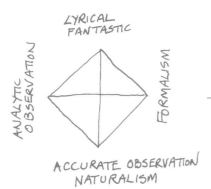

Each discipline has a code. To work in a discipline it is necessary to learn the code. The Uniform Building Code controls the basic essentials of sound construction practice within a specific region. The layout of this book is based on a code established by graphic designers as an effective way to relay information. Codes may be referred to as styles, movements, schools of thought, and so on. All such codes imply frameworks in which to operate. Modernism, for example, embodies tenets or codes that must be followed for the work to be seen as "modern."

Individuals suggest changes to the existing codes. New codes spawn new signs that represent the code. The Arts and Crafts thinkers John Ruskin and William Morris advocated simplification in the design of everyday objects; the Bauhaus advocated strengthening the relationship between the arts and industry; Mies van der Rohe coined the phrase "less is more." Modernity evolves. Each new player adds his or her own perceptions, some ideas take

communicating. When the information is more difficult and unconventional, it is concerned with subject. The simple communication is likely to be an attempt to maintain the status quo and opposed to change. The new is uncomfortable, even shocking, and harder to communicate. New art forms eventually become familiar and generally accepted by everybody. The Impressionist painters, Gerrit Rietveld furniture, the electric or propane car, and the green design of Victor Papanek have all become generally accepted.

Before meaning can be established, external stimuli must be matched with the internal patterns of the mind. These internal patterns are the result of cultural experience. One culture is different from another; different cultures equal different realities. Some psychological and physiological aspects, such as gender and orientation, will also impinge on the person's experience but how to work with these is informed largely by the dictates of current cultural norms.

LYRICAL/FANTASTIC

FORMALISM

ACCURATE OBSERVATION/NATURALISM

ANALYTIC OBSERVATION

> ...the past, since it cannot be really destroyed,...must be revisited: but with irony, not innocently.
>
> ∽
> UMBERTO ECCO

root in the culture and become beacons to follow. Styles such as Impressionism, Art Nouveau, and Art Deco are explored until they become familiar, whereupon they no longer hold fascination for the creative mind. Working within the code is important, changing an aspect or a specific sign is expected. Only rarely does a code change completely, and it takes many people to agree that this is appropriate.

A code assists communication to those who want to understand how something is done. A code may be used to control by those who can decode it. Every profession has developed a code of signs that its initiates guard. The early guilds treated their knowledge with great secrecy; in these more enlightened times information is shared freely but nevertheless codes are used to guard quality. These codes are often technical rather than aesthetic. Building codes, for example, are quite firm even as they evolve to deal with new materials and new safety criteria. The computer has codes and special language that have to be learned before the simplest tasks can be discussed.

The International Standards Organization attempts to ease communication between countries and cultures by setting up common symbolic languages, such as the road signs and travel signs. Modernism has a code, as does Structuralism and every other "ism." Some codes require deciphering and two people may well share parts but disagree on others, all subject to change at any moment. While we try to guard quality through legislated or generally agreed codes, the nature of the creative experience and of appearance suggest that continual critical appraisal is most important.

IMAGE MAKING OVERVIEW

Image making may fall broadly into the categories LYRICAL and FANTASTIC, ACCURATE OBSERVATIONS, FORMALISM and beauty, or ANALYTIC OBSERVA-TIONS. While these four may not include all forms of

> I don't want realism. I want magic...I don't tell truth, I tell what ought to be truth.
>
> ∽
> TENNESSEE WILLIAMS
> A STREETCAR NAMED DESIRE

representation, they will launch us into the sea of images and objects with a map.

First, a comment on **REPRESENTATION** and why that term has not been used for the heading of this section. Representation is a word that has picked up so many meanings that it can confuse rather than clarify. If the word is broken down as **RE-PRESENT** the meaning becomes apparent. A **PRESENT** is something given but to re-present is to give something again, a lecture or a sales pitch for example. To **REPRESENT** something is to act as a conduit between two people, as a mediator and explainer. **REPRESENTATIONAL** works depict a place, person, or thing, and the objects and subjects are generally recognizable. **ABSTRACTION** represents nothing except the artist's interests, and is outside the study of representation and iconography. Image is inclusive and relates to the human imagination. Any work has an image, though it is not necessarily a representation of something else. Aircraft, painting, the architectural detail of a newel-post, ceramic and wood vessels, installation art, all become images created from the imagination. They all communicate information about the culture in which they were created.

ACCURATE OBSERVATION

Accurate observation is often referred to as **NATURALISM** or **REALISM**. It is a means to re-present or represent what we see with a high degree of accuracy. The idea of accuracy is flawed because when a person or thing is translated from one material to another, inevitable changes have taken place. The body carved in wood lacks the subtlety of flesh, even if the wood grain interacts wonderfully

> The Power of Myth—People say that what we're all seeking is a meaning for life. I think that what we're really seeking is the experience of being alive so that our life experiences on purely physical plane will have resonances within our innermost being and reality, so that we actually feel the rapture of being alive.
>
> ✧
> JOSEPH CAMPBELL

with the form. What is suggested by the juxtaposition of flesh with wood grain? Accuracy is lost in the translation, but something else is implied that has the potential of being more interesting. Too much attention to accuracy may objectify what is looked at, squeezing out the emotions or feelings of the artist and transmitting nothing to the viewer of the excitement of life. Realism may convey a high level of commitment because of the fidelity of the image; unfortunately, many people are stuck in realism. They have little appreciation for anything that does not represent something else. Whether accurate observation is a restricted code or a broadcast code, the intent is to reach a mass audience, a broad cross-section of people. An elaborated code or narrowcast code is focused on a specific group or community of people.

In advertising for Benetton, the artist Oliviero Toscani has communicated contemporary social issues. Three faces stare back, each with their tongues poking out at the viewer. The children are from three distinct races but each has a tongue the same color. The title of the image is *United Colors of Toscani.* Accurate observations can be problematic. Innocence has been portrayed to support the most terrible tyrannies of Fascism. What is reliable knowledge in issues of race? How is innocence used? The Benetton advertising is clever in its humanity—children are a delight, the message is clear, we need to enjoy our racial diversity together. Meanwhile it also boosts sales. Accuracy of image is one aspect, what about accuracy of values in the subject, and accuracy in the context in which the children are used?

The fidelity of realism heightens the nuances offered by accurate observation, but it needs extreme care. By noting the exceptional quality or character of the subject, the realistic becomes more real. Reality and truth become uncomfortable partners when we rigidly stick to confining definitions. The subtle exaggeration of reality makes the form appear super-real, hence Surrealism, which focuses our attention in unexpected ways. The shifting and interpreting of

For the "message" of any medium or technology is the change of scale or pace or pattern that it introduces into human affairs.

☙

MARSHALL MCLUHAN

reality focuses the viewer on the subject of the work rather than presenting only an objectified and unfeeling, unthinking and mechanical view. Interpretation and nuance are everything.

FORMALISM AND BEAUTY

Formalism is concerned with the form or design of something but it is not necessarily about beauty. Well, it may be, but we seem unable to define beauty since the inception of philosophy, so I shall not attempt it here. ABSTRACTION is concerned with essence. An abstract work will attempt to bring out the essence or spirit of the subject, and reveal it with all the directness that abstraction can offer. Henry Moore and Barbara Hepworth both presented abstract work based on forms found in nature. They studied BIOMORPHIC or ORGANIC form to discover the poetic and profound truth of its beauty. The beauty they discovered can be quite rugged, even disconcerting, in its directness; unlike idealized forms that have been polished to remove the truth of the materials, the structures of life, and the abrasions of reality.

If we take a quick glance at something we receive its GESTALT. The gestalt refers to the outline

Deception and irony are neighbors. In deception, the reality is withheld. In irony, it is implicit.

☙

CAROLYN BELL FARRELL

The Move
1990

Woven tapestry—wool on
cotton warp
184 x 184 cm
Sue Brinkhurst
Sussex, UK

Who and what gets represented in The Move? The artist is an observer making an accurate emotional observation about the unnerving chaos of moving. What looks like the partner on the bottom, dressed as Harlequin, juggles child, pets, teapot, cleaning materials, a chair on which to relax and read the book, and a clock (at the top of the frame) with all its implications. The shapes (which are flat and simplified) catch and rattle next to the zig zag of the perimeter. The balance between figure and ground is about equal and the objects begin to have a similar visual weight, which adds to the confusion of relative importance. Sue Brinkhurst comments: *"In the Comedia del'Arte, the Harlequin was often called upon to 'fill in' roles and needed the capabilities to represent a diverse repertoire of characters, unlike the other actors who tended to specialize in one particular role. As a mother, wife, artist, housewife, etc, my roles too are multi-functional and so the figure is more a representation of myself than of my partner!"*

120

or surface tension of the object; it senses and feels what is there. It may be an ideal way of seeing because the harshness of reality can be left out. Conversely, all our attention may be focused on the specific reality or issue at hand. It is the removal of nonessentials. There is an abstracting of the form, though it is not strictly speaking abstraction. A face with all its complexity can be reduced to an oval that is an abstraction, but at what point, as we add the features, does the oval evolve into a representation of a specific person?

Abstraction may also be recognizable as a concern for line, form, space, color, and the emotional response to the purity of these elements. **NONOBJECTIVE** or **NONREPRESENTATIONAL** forms refer to nothing that is concrete or recognizable. If a form has an organic shape but it is nonspecific, it is an abstraction that may be referred to as **BIOMORPHIC**. When there is no specific intention to represent something then the work is nonobjective. Often abstraction is referred to as **GEOMETRIC** or **HARD-EDGED** and associated with math, science, and rationality. There is no reason to re-present except to present itself, and the

viewer then has to respond to the qualities of line, pattern, composition, and materials. That is the subject, and the artist draws all our focus to the creation of the project. The **CONSTRUCTIVISTS** worked entirely with nonobjective forms; at the turn of the last century, the painters Wasily Kandinsky and Natalia Goncharova created with pure form and design as a reaction to the dominant realism of their academic past.

LYRICAL AND FANTASTIC

There are widely different means of representing the subject. A street sign indicates what is to be done and there is no doubt about the intention of the message. Another image may be baffling on first encounter but it is strong enough to make us pause or return to discover more. Other images confound our understanding, but still draw us closer to knowing because of our previous deliberations on the subject represented. Lyrical forms were used by the architect Eero Saarinen in the Dulles Airport in 1961-2. Long graceful curves articulate the space with a wonderful sense of flight. The paintings of Georgia O'Keeffe are huge representations of plant and flower forms. Their

And this our life, exempt from public hauny,
Find tongues in trees, books in the running brooks,
Sermons in stones, and good in everything.

☙

SHAKESPEARE
AS YOU LIKE IT, ACT II, SCENE 1

blake debosegai

Dorothy C
1992

20 x 16"
Acrylic on canvas
Blake Debosegai
Manitoulin Island, Ontario, Canada

Blake Debosegai writes, *"Dorothy Corbiere was a close friend who passed away three years ago at the age of 60. To have someone that is special and lose that person leaves you feeling empty and hurt. For someone to lose a partner, the pain must be unbearable. But Dorothy and I had a long relationship, from the time I was a child until I was a teen she would sit us. When I grew older I worked with her on her quilts by supplying patterns. She would also ask me to create certain designs. She told me that her favorite creature on this earth was the chick-a-dee. She said she just loved to hear them sing and they looked beautiful. She would say, 'When I die I'm going to come back as a chick-a-dee, flying around and go wherever I wish. I'll come and visit you.'*

"The other powerful memory I have of Dorothy is of a black-and-white photograph that she had in her house, of a pretty thirteen-year-old Ojibwe girl from the Georgian Bay coast, visiting on Manitoulin Island. It was her."

Representation is complex. Within any image numerous layers of representation are present and presented. What and who is represented in Blake Debosegai's Dorothy C? The work is titled Dorothy C yet the primary form represented is a chickadee in a tree. While Dorothy C is the subject, Debosegai's story is about his feelings and represents the way he sees the subject. Dorothy Corbiere and chickadee merge and present the idea of animism—the bird becoming the disembodied spirit of Dorothy, elegantly transformed by the artist's imagination and brush.

The stylization of the image is typical of the Woodland artists of Manitoulin Island, among whom Debosegai is a leader. Most of these artists are from the Ojibwe tribe of First Nation people. The work is unmistakably a representation by a Woodland artist. The mythologizing of the chickadee has been represented many times before in different ways. The year before Debosegai had painted a representation titled Origins of the Chick-a-Dee. In Dorothy C he takes the original myth and re-presents aspects within the context of his own personal mythology. For the artist, culture is organic and living—the representation always transforming.

Dorothy C is a deeply felt story of relationships, simultaneously simple and complex, specific and common to the human experience. But writing about the work I am in the dangerous position of potentially misrepresenting the artist's image, even appropriating the image to represent my point of view, in order to open a discussion on representation. These comments reveal a few of the complexities of appearance, of who is represented and what is communicated, in contemporary society.

scale, luxuriant form, and color place them between the lyrical and fantastic. Marisol Escobar, who was associated with the Pop artists, takes the familiar and transforms it into satirical images. The fantastic is well served by Salvador Dali, whose dream-like images transform into nightmares.

In the 20th century, the artist has wanted viewers to apprehend the project and reach their own conclusions. There is an expectation that viewers will think about what they are looking at, rather than just doing what the sign says. Receiving the full implication and meaning of an obscure metaphor requires more knowledge and perhaps an imaginative leap. 20th century art is often **PARADOXICAL** beyond belief, self-contradictory, and **AMBIGUOUS**.

Symbols and allegories were used extensively prior to the Industrial Revolution; Modernism has often used the metaphor to create meaning; Post-Modernism presents images that mediate between the subject and the viewer. The sign directed the viewer, the allegory instructed the follower, the metaphor involved the viewer in the creation of the idea, and mediation enables the artist's project to act as a conduit for the viewer to comprehend that which is outside his or her experience. Through these means the artist's work lyrically express thoughts or fantasies conjured from the imagination.

ANALYTIC OBSERVER

The analytic observer decodes before encoding. The idea tends to be more important. The accurate observer will tend to be more interested in the outward appearance, while the analytic observer is more interested in what is behind the appearance. The appearance is a sign in a code that questions and expands communication and understanding.

The project with the greatest depth tends to be analytic; perhaps all the great projects have been analytic. As feminism emerged in the last 40 years it has been extremely analytic of structures of behavior. Some of this work is political to its root, while some references the politics of gender in a subtle manner. Jackie Windsor has wrapped copper around a wood stick to form what looks like a ball of wool prepared by a hand knitter. The image of a ball of wool is strongly associated with women. There are two balls of wool to each stick and 36 sticks that stand vertically, forming a cube-like piece. This work is quietly evocative. In contrast, the installations of Jamelie Hassan are more directly political. However, Hassan avoids didactic rhetorical instructions and presents the project in such a way that the viewer has to come to terms with his or her own understanding of the issues. In her installation *Meeting Nasser*, three photographs show a young girl presenting the political and military entourage with a bouquet of wrapped flowers. A video screen in front of these images shows a young girl returning in a dress of another color. The viewer is encouraged to think why, to feel the experience of the child, and to ask what in the bigger picture this may mean.

A sign is a significant mark with special meaning. A sign may be a board with an image that communicates a simple message. For some, a sign may come from a divine power, revealed through natural phenomena. For our purposes it is essential to deconstruct all signs and images to see what they really communicate, who is communicating, and to what ends the communications are put.

The analytic observer uses any tool that will help access a greater knowledge of the subject and context. Science has invested enormous energy in new ways of seeing. Perhaps the most stunning example from this century is the image of the Earth as seen from the Moon.

DESCRIPTIVE DEVICES

The SYMBOL represents something else—an idea or a quality. An X + # or cross are all simple variations of intersecting lines, but each acts as a symbol with particular meaning. Any symbol will have a variety of meanings that depend upon its context, which may be a social group, nation, religion, and so on. A tree may represent life, knowledge, good and evil, or it may be a regional emblem on a crest. Certain forms seem to have authenticity in the **COLLECTIVE UNCONSCIOUS.** Carl Jung identified as symbols of our emotional concerns the images that come to us from the unconscious in dreams or spontaneously in relaxed moments. Artists often present images like these. Society has seen these images, and has constructed belief systems around them, often as a means to control or instruct people in ways of doing things or of seeing the world. Conversely, the artist, craftsperson, designer, or scientist works toward the common goal with complicity, not questioning the motive of the group. Within the symbolic framework various "devices" may be used, such as **ALLEGORIES** in painting, which enable the telling of stories. The **NARRATIVE** is strengthened by the **IMAGE,** which often is easier to remember and to identify with than the abstract idea.

The **METAPHOR,** unlike the allegory, does not tell a story. A metaphor is a description of one thing in terms of another. A glaring error does not really glare, but we know what it means because we have seen the glare of the sun off the water. Modernism has worked with the metaphor as a means of bringing a heightened sense of mystery to the familiar. A crumbling form will be a metaphor for spiritual decay, a circular table will be a metaphor for communications and the possibility of peace.

The sign **DIRECTS** the viewer, the allegory **INSTRUCTS** the follower, the metaphor **INVOLVES** the viewer in the creation of the idea, and mediation **ENABLES** the artist's project to act as a conduit for the viewer to comprehend that which is outside his or her experience. The idea has become central to the project—the sensory delight in materiality is secondary.

CONCLUSION

Images are not always pat, straightforward, and an easy read that communicates new **KNOWLEDGE,** nor a sign that directly instructs. On occasion an image pinned down with a label may lose much of its attraction. The label should launch the viewer in the direction of the image's underpinning. It should not necessarily be an explanation. The reflective inquiry and the questions raised in the viewer are what is engaging. A strong image is dense with evocative and sometimes provocative meanings. Strength may be achieved through ambiguous images and the juxtaposition of unexpected elements. Poetic ambiguity leads the viewer toward the pleasures of **KNOWING.** This intuitive knowing becomes the foundation for knowledge of the subject. In this we can see, with or through the artist, the world in which we live. The know-how of communication and representation is the ability to work within the different codes of each discipline.

CHAPTER EIGHT

**Magdalene Bridge,
Cambridge, Victory Row Past**
1995

Acrylic / pen on paper
21 x 31"
Liz Moon
Cambridge, Suffolk, UK

Magdalene Bridge represents a community of people. The painter may be part of this community or entirely an observer. The image implicates the artist as part of the community because she sits in the boathouse or restaurant looking out at the scullers passing beneath the bridge. There is also humor for those familiar with the space. The "Victory Row Past" is a "why not" possibility, for a reach of the river usually inhabited only by punts.

The artist is no different from others who enjoy the experiences of working together to relax in exercise. Liz Moon studied engineering at Oxford University and in Magdalene Bridge her interest in engineering is still evident in the detailing of the bridge.

The image is concerned with space and movement—people in action, fluidity of line, and the transparency of color make the work transient, yet alive. Some elements appear unfinished, enabling the viewer to feel part of the process, to be in on the completion of boat race and painting. Water color techniques compared to oil paints are often rapid and spontaneous, with the aesthetic of the sketch. We feel closer to the experience of perception because the work is not labored but celebrates empathetically the experience of this community.

Community

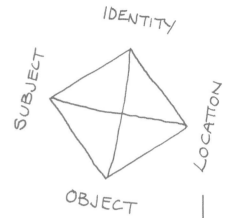

OVERVIEW

We all belong to different communities, some we are born into and some we choose. We appear in relationship to others of similar appearance, skills, and attitudes. Equally (and probably healthier) we appear together with others of dissimilar appearance. Dissimilarity forms a richness of diversity, where one can help another to produce a whole community. Our realities ultimately are formed at the junctions of dissimilarity.

FIT AND LOOSE FIT

There are few hermits and many communities. How each person fits is vital to the survival of both the individual and of the community. Most of us belong to several communities. Some will fit into a leadership role while others develop a more tentative or loose fit as observers. Some may be motivated by a sense of belonging or a need to affiliate for a particular cause. Fit, loose fit, and misfit are three relationships that the individual may experience with a community. The last chapter discussed object and subject relations. The subject of the object and where it is located will eventually become the identity of the individual and the community.

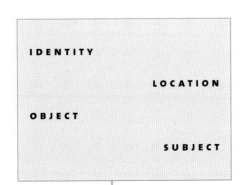

Raymond Williams makes the case for inter-related practice in one of his essays:

"The fatally wrong approach, to any such study, is from the assumption of separate orders, as when we ordinarily assume that political institutions and conventions are of a different and separate order from artistic institutions and conventions. Politics and art, together with science, religion, family life and other categories we speak of as absolutes, belong in a whole world of active and interactive relationships... If we begin from the whole texture, we can go on to study particular activities, and their bearings on other kinds. Yet we begin, normally, from the categories themselves, and this has led again and again to a damaging suppression of relationships."

A sense of one's racial and cultural background, like a sense of one's personal likes and dislikes, is essential to an individual sense of self. But neither history nor race nor culture is destiny: human beings are saved from that by intelligence and the gift of irony. And it is the ironic eye, questioning, judging, that ultimately refuses to simplify.

&

NEIL BISSOONDATH

LOCATION AND SUBJECT

There are many ways to identify community but the simplest is based in **LOCATION** of **SUBJECT**. The town I live in is one community (location). I belong to the local gallery where I can see the work of landscape painters (location and subject). I am interested in talking to painters about their landscapes and their inspirations for the images (subject). The location of the subject is in the artist's painting. What the artist thinks and feels about the place is located in the work—in the painting—and is the identity and content of the work.

LOCATION AND IDENTITY

The idea of a region may be about location—that is, geographic—or identity—that is, community. Another way of looking at community is to think about **LOCATION** and **IDENTITY** as inseparable. We identify with the subject being investigated; the communities we join or interact with help develop our identity. The subject we think about helps locate our identity just as much as where we physically live. Mentally and physically, we live in locations.

There have always been many relational communities but in recent years our society has focused on the problems and relationships involved with **AGE, GENDER, ORIENTATION, RACE,** and **RELIGION**. You can see that our identities are strongly linked to these terms: our age (young, middle aged, old); gender (male, female); orientation (heterosexual, bisexual, homosexual); race (ethnic origin or origins); religion (belief system). Each of these terms represents a community of people that one does not necessarily have a membership in, or a choice about, but inevitably there are implications for us in the "belonging." Appearance does not necessarily follow a logical response in our social reality. As Dan Gardner reports in The Globe and Mail (Oct 21 1995), "So few genetic differences exist between blacks and whites that biologists believe the concept of race is meaningless. But as a social idea, it is alive and thriving..."

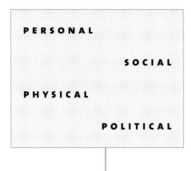

Communities of age, gender, orientation, race, and religion may be difficult to see in relation to the productive life of the maker, designer, or artist. Each of us (knowingly or unknowingly) creates within our own genre. Rap reggae, punk, rock, folk, and so on all carry their own aesthetic baggage. More traditionally, religion has developed ceremonies that use objects such as the processional cross to present the specific concepts of the belief system. Fred Wilson, in a project called *Mining the Museum*, prepared an installation about issues of race. In the installation *Metal Work 1793 - 1880,* silver vessels were presented along with shackles worn by slaves. Wilson's provocative political juxtaposition presented different realities not usually seen at the museum. Instead of stuff in cases, albeit exquisitely beautiful stuff, the museum curator has the opportunity to reevaluate the stories around each project, extending its life beyond the sensual to include the social and the political.

There are many other communities to which we may belong: a bridge club, life-drawing class, basketball team, association of anglers, group of

environmentalists. Some communities will affect our identities more strongly than others. The traditional quilters working together develop designs for their families and community. For hundreds of years, useful and beautiful bed coverings have been created by these loosely associated communities. By comparison, in 1997 the Louisville Slugger Museum along with the makers of Louisville Slugger baseball bats presented an exhibition called Bats and Bowls. People were selected from the woodturning community for their imaginative approach to the traditionally stiff and formal approach of that craft. An imaginative, silly, wonderful, extraordinary and precocious exhibition brought new life to the idea of baseball bats and turned bowls. Communities of expertise and skill can move together, making their identities through playful caring and serious activities.

REPRESENTATION

Representation is complex and problematic. Who represents what? Do we have the right to represent anything other than ourselves? Taking and using

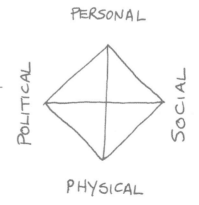

Confessional
1995

Monoprint—oil paint on paper
31 x 30 cm
Pat Waters
Briagolong, Victoria, Australia

Pat Waters uses paint to draw images. Working this way gives the work an immediacy. It is as if the painter is in a hurry to communicate the subject matter. Sometimes this can leave the content of the work as a quick read like an advertisement, with not much to contemplate or discover. The work is allegorical eveles' a human

conduct or experience. Waters has a background in the peace movement. Her images often are concerned with the physical and emotional interactions of people in moments of high stress, crisis and tragic brutal deaths. Of this work Waters has written, "...*myths increasingly fascinate me, why the allegory contained within them becomes*

clearer as time passes and why drawing and painting them is becoming more personally relevant."

Within community we need images to guide our collective interactions. Often, the only images we see publicly are advertisements. The works of Pat Waters suggest an approach to communicating other community concerns

somebody else's image is called appropriation. It can be a theft from the other person or from their culture. Perhaps the representation is of a perception or a concept. It is not precisely about ourselves or about somebody else.

COMMUNITY ECOLOGY

For appearance we will look at four broad areas that influence any community. These are the POLITICAL, PERSONAL, SOCIAL, and PHYSICAL spheres.

By POLITICAL, we mean how we govern our communities, the laws of behavior such as free speech and who gets represented by whom. When a person is represented in an image, what does it do to that person? Does it show him or her in a light that is fair, appropriate, intelligent and caring? Or are the individual's rights violated? The photographer whose work appears in mass media must address concerns about how the individual is represented. We each have responsibilities to see that the political system and the way we organize our society is nurtured at the very least by voting and following the laws of the land. The architect and builder must know and obey the many codes developed to give us the freedom to live safely and in harmony. A sidewalk of regulation width does, after all, allow comfortable and considerate passing. The designer will on occasion offer his or her skills to politically motivated groups, believing the cause is worthwhile and ultimately beneficial to the whole of society. Conversely, the project of artists like Barbara Kruger and Jenny Holzer is to shock the politically lazy into seeing see in a fresh way how we are organizing values in the larger community.

The PERSONAL appearance acts out our own identity. Everybody needs to be seen and identified within his or her chosen community. Conversely, everybody needs to have a personal or private life. The personal may well be the hermetic experience of contemplation, where identity is nurtured by the individual and not controlled by the community. It is within the (en)close(d) relation of immediate family and household that ethnicity, for example, can be best experienced. Ethnicity or race belongs to the individual and not to the community. When a community vehemently claims race, it tends toward racism and war. The objects people make, like their spoken language, express the dreams, aspirations, visions, and meanings at the moment of making. The objects I have made for my family do to a large extent represent my family interests and relationships. The making and expressing of home life spills into the maker's other communities, and ultimately into the public realm. Therefore for some the appearance of what is made will reflect the inner life of the maker and his or her relationship with the chosen community.

> It's most powerful to be on the margin. You can always jump into the center but you don't stay there because then everybody knows where to get you. You stay on the outside, because that's how you survive.
>
> JANE ASH POITRAS

Burning Labyrinth
1991

Beach sand, paper, sawdust
and kerosene
50' x 50'
Miz-Maze Theatre—John
Anderson, Nancy Bertelsen, Mary
Eubank, Tim Graveson, Zea
Morvitz, Edward Sexton, Karen
Sexton, and Patti Trimble
Marin County, California, USA

Mary Eubank was one of the
founders of Gallery Route One in
Marin County and has worked on a
number of collaborative projects.
She has written, *"Miz-Maze Theater
is committed to a collaborative and
interdisciplinary approach to
installation and theater. It is critical
in collaboration to work with people
who have a similar guiding impulse
and notion of the structure of
consciousness in order to be able to
work through the problems of ego,
aesthetic preferences, trust,
boundaries, emotional
temperaments, anxiety, etc. All of
these issues emerge in the process of
working with other artists
collaboratively, but that is one of the
interesting elements of the process.
The alchemical lies within the
collaborative process; that is, the
combination of various ideas,
temperaments, and energies, the
'heating' of them together in the
alchemical furnace of the
collaborative process, produces
something which is a unique
combination of these separate
elements and individuals.*

*"Miz-Maze has also worked
extensively with the labyrinth form,
and the concept of the library as a
labyrinth of knowledge... The
internet, for example, can be
understood as a vast global
labyrinth or maze."*

Place is the physical, the location of old identities; Space is where the activity takes place and new identities form; Time enables and matures identity; Context and juxtaposition are the nexus for identity.

☙

But not always, since some designers direct their personal expressive vision toward what they believe is the collective good. A highway sign emphatically does not need to be personalized or expressive, just legible at high speed in a blizzard. Equally, personal space hardly needs Modernist aesthetics instead of the elements that help synthesize the household. The SOCIAL connection to like-minded communities may take the form of a sports club or environmental group, a school or university. These associations do not much care about age, gender, orientation, race, or religion, but rather, how one plays the game or one's abilities within the subject of interest. Within these social groups or communities, the needs and desires of the group get worked out in a mutual exchange. The appearance of the group is determined from the inside out. Inevitably the representation of the community is reformed after exposure to another team or community. It is an evolving collective appearance. Identities form in the spaces where communities interact. It is the acting out itself that forms the identity.

A person's social interactions take place in semi-private places such as the church hall or private club, or in public places in a semi-private manner, such as at the art gallery, library, or community center. Membership is often a prerequisite for interaction, but usually it is open to most people. Occasionally the interests of a social group spills into the public consciousness. Festivals and events establish shared interest and offer opportunities, for example, to graphic designers in the promotion of Carabana, a parade with a Caribbean history, and to costume artists to go fabulously wild. On rare occasions places become a more permanent expressions of a group, for example, the Fifth Season Cycle Center in Owen Sound, a partnership of private and public organizations who have identified a common good that changes the physical space of the larger community (page 136).

The PHYSICAL location houses the activity, which inevitably influences the appearance. The activity becomes defined and needs a field for its appearance. The first game of football did not need a stadium but the game is now so wrapped up with its appearance that the activity demands a greater sense of place. Some governments and religions have made the grand appearance a great outward show, while others have been more restrained, contemplative, inward, and reflective. The physical place and its appearance may strongly represent power relations within the community. While

My work is not made for Indian people but for thinking people. In the global and evolutionary scheme, the difference between humans is negligible.

☙

CARL BEAM

artists, designers and makers look for work at these places, the technologists and scientists scoop up most of the available funds building bigger and occasionally better places. Organizations, especially those with huge profits, tend to take on impressive physical appearances.

PLACE, SPACE, AND TIME

Place is the location, and space is where the ACT, ACTION, and ACTIVITY "takes place." The "taking of place" can be a reinforcing of its history, a reinterpretation of existing perceptions, or a rewriting of the story about the location and its identity. Over time the appearance of a place changes by physical transformation or simply by the way people look at it—PERCEPTION changes with familiarity. Walking in the woods for the first time is quite different from the one hundredth walk, when all the plants and animals can be recognized, named, and seen in the context of an active ecology.

Sometimes a writer or a painter may represent place in an unexpected manner; this may become an unusual identity that sticks, whereupon people will think about the place in that FRAMED CONTEXT. New Orleans is a place for great jazz played on the street and in the bars. But that is only a very small part of the city's life. It is possible to live in New Orleans and never go to the district that is known around the world for its music.

Another city may have a vibrant Chinatown—colorful, festive, and filled with images of imperial China. This Chinatown has less to do with its host town than with another place and time. It is possible to walk through without putting on the costume, without identifying with the dominant culture of place, and yet the act of walking through the space changes. I may even live in Chinatown but choose not to wear its costume, not to entertain the expectations of tourists.

People's IDENTITIES evolve through their actions. New identities often take place slowly, but sometimes emerge with a shock, like the recent fashion for cropped, parrot-colored hair. Even a commuter repeating the same journey over and over changes identity as the time of day, months, and years wear on. The commuter grows older; the advertisements are presented more to the regular commuter than to the casual traveler. The demographics of the rider and of the advertisements form a union. Over the years the place will change because the people have changed. A ride on the underground 30 years ago is strikingly different from a ride today. Fashions in clothing, colors of the trains, kinds of advertisements are all culturally evolving, creating a new place with new identities.

For the identity of the individual to evolve, he or she needs space in which to act. The fixedness of place is the backdrop for what people do, who they want to be; their aspirations can be enabled by the space. A good library will want the person to grow and take over the library as his or her own. The

> We're living in the ruins of bygone communities, in special-interest networks that aren't really communities at all—they're ghettos of like-minded people.
>
> ⸎
> ERIC UTNE

books must reflect the users' interests, then they in effect take over the place by using the space. The larger society needs the place to present a certain level of COLLECTIVE IDENTITY. A city may have a library, art gallery, and several museums, which together reflect the community's identity. Politicians and tourist boards are acutely aware of these cultural assets and are forever trying to sell the image of the place rather than the use of the space. What has to be identified is the activity in the place and who will animate the space. What, then, are the social and cultural processes and activities that inform identity? Which activities best inform our identities? The space must first be imagined—all cultural activity has to be imagined and the politician is the last person who should take on that job. Next, the space must be imaginatively arranged before the place can be constructed. Only then can the space be activated with activities that nurture our identities.

NURTURING CULTURE

Like gardens, most communities need to be tended. Communities usually do not grow randomly in the wild, but under supervision. At least, one hopes the vision is super. A garden is a community of plants. Vegetables, like people, grow in soil that has to be worked; we need to feed them, weed them, and protect them from predators. Properly developed, a garden can become self organizing with the minimum of maintenance—at least that is the

objective in my garden. A computer is a community of components. It is vital that their interrelation be harmonious, for the overall function of the machine depends on the reality of those relationships. Culture is a TAMED BEHAVIOR, we hope of exquisitely refined relationships, only occasionally rebellious—even if one of the disciplines appears to be testing the limits of perception. The tamed behavior and its appearance works better because of its COMPASSION and ability to make life less brutish and demanding. Life with moments of DIVERSITY, LEISURE and INSIGHT seems ideal and is often the subject of appearance. The novelist Margaret Atwood once pointed out that creatures who do not see their reflection in a mirror are vampires: empty beings who merely feed on others. Individuals and communities need to construct their appearance so that we can see ourselves as well as those around us. The AUTHENTICITY of the individual's voice in the community best expresses our collective imagination and the faith we need to survive in a cooperative and collective way.

Certain activities need a community of people or a committee to balance the outspoken or, more importantly, to offer increased expertise in the face

Fifth Season Cycle Centre
1994

Multi Media
14' x 50' x 50'
Eric Clough, Andrew Goss,
Stephen Hogbin, Jim Hong Louie,
Robert Osthoff
Grey County, Ontario, Canada

This installation was the collaboration of several communities, including the artists who created the work, cyclists who were planning new cycle routes for the city, and the umbrella group for the project—the Owen Sound Round Table on the Economy and Environment. Other communities included downtown business people, the art gallery, and various city departments. Some projects require the collaboration and cooperation of many people. There were many planning meetings to discuss the idea of the project and the issues of constructing it. The artists were involved at every stage of the process. The team of artists had four planning meetings which covered the initial discussion of the concept, implications of the word "cycles," agreement concerning responsibilities, the site plan and the location of each artist's work. Models were assembled into the maquette. Next we reviewed what had been made, redesigned and costed the project. Eventually presentations were made to City Council, and to the interested public. On approval the work was carried out by the artists with some assistance from local industries. The Fifth Season Cycle Centre is both functional and symbolic of the relationship among various communities and the environment.

> Between totalitarian order and anarchy lie reasonable social and political systems and the best of them encompass a peak of ordered diversity.
>
> ❧
>
> MICHAEL MCGUIRE

of COMPLEXITY. A film crew or architect's partnership both work as a team in order to realize the appearance. Scientists in laboratories around the world work together toward common understanding of complex issues.

Regardless of the artist's or actor's performance the presence of the audience is essential. How can the artist survive without interplay?

RIGHTS AND RESPONSIBILITIES

The creator of an image, object, place, or space has certain rights and responsibilities. At one end of the scale the LIMITATIONS OF RESPONSIBILITY are almost removed to allow FREEDOM OF EXPRESSION for the individual. Art and to some degree pure science are about the explorations by the individual into new territories. At the other end a creator may work entirely to fulfill his or her RESPONSIBILITIES TO THE COMMUNITY. The wheelchair designer may have no need for a wheelchair but is drawn to work toward solutions for others. The community has a responsibility to look after the individual in his or her specific quest, even though the available resources are limited. It becomes vital to see each situation in the proper context. If it is all individualistic and CARELESS OF THE SPECIES, we know from nature

that survival is drastically reduced. Some would argue the extreme, that the individual is expendable, but even that argument seems flawed. DIVERSITY, BALANCE, UNITY, and HARMONY are all essential for survival. As Jane Jacobs points out in *The Death and Life of Great American Cities*, the life on a Greenwich Village street appears as *"an intricate ballet in which the individual dancers and ensembles all have distinctive parts (that) miraculously reinforce each other and compose an orderly whole."*

CONCLUSION

From the dance on the street at the local level to the World Wide Web and its international embrace through the specificity of interest, we find new and ever-expanding communities. Global and virtual communities can never quite replace local ones. The local culture and its parochial impulse to be closed to new possibilities, and the large community's imperialist tendency to control it neighbors, are both tendencies to be avoided. The human story suggests that to be one or the other is destructive, while a balanced curiosity with lots of empathy for the other goes a long way toward creating vibrant and healthy communities.

The creative person has rights and responsibilities to develop himself or herself in relationship to the community. The individual grows from the family or household into the specialty group and community in a never-ending cycle of taking and receiving, massaging, and giving. The appearance that develops may not always be the most exciting, but it is entirely reasonable and responsible. It has relevance and bears the marks of TRUTH TO CONTEXT AND COMMUNITY.

Region

**Canadology:
Rite of Winter Solstice
1988**

57 x 50"
Acrylic on Canvas
John B. Boyle
Bruce County, Ontario, Canada

John B. Boyle is an painter with a passion for national and regional concerns. His recent work presents a series of images and stories called "The Canadology Series." These are stories of the imagination—*"tales of an antediluvian nation called Canada (which) have recurred in the lore of the ancient civilization."* Situated next to the painted image is a text:

"In winter, then as now, everything is black and white deep in the forest, though the grays between can be every shade and hue. Each December 21st, Canadians would celebrate the end of the season of color and the beginning of the season of black and white and myriad grays with the rite of winter solstice. Singly they stole, by the light of the moon, naked, into the depths of the forests to their birth tress, a tree selected at birth to be theirs and theirs alone, repository of the spirit, giver of energy, keeper of the secret. The exact nature of the rite is not known. Often keepers of the rite did not emerge from the groves till dawn. There were occasionally cases of mortality in severe weather, the supplicants found bonded to their sacred trees. In later years the Royal Canadian Mounted Police and the Secret Service made concerted efforts to stamp out the practice, with indifferent results."

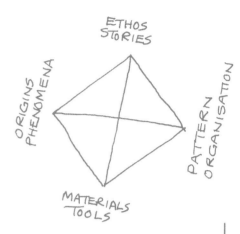

OVERVIEW

Where we live and the appearance of a region is fundamental to the experience of most people. Only a very few people live a truly international life. The region informs us through physical appearance, the stories of place, how we are organized, and the phenomena of site. Usually the most successful work resonates with our sense of place because it is, after all, what we know best. Occasionally a person will be entranced by the exotic and the Other from away, when the same experience may equally be found in one's own region.

BETWEEN MACRO AND MICRO VIEWS

Why choose regionalism over nationalism or internationalism? Living in a region will guide us at the local, national, and international levels. It is the place where both the macro and the micro views can be seen most vividly in action. The region is neither so big that it lies beyond our immediate experience, nor so small that we miss the big picture.

THE CITY AS REGION

Some regions are known for their produce, such as apples or grapes, while others, like the Canadian prairies, for their livestock and grain. Cities will take on characteristics often associated

ETHOS — STORIES

PATTERN — ORGANIZATION

MATERIALS — TOOLS

ORIGINS — PHENOMENA

with their industries or with the arts, for example the architecture of Chicago or the fashions from Paris, while Rome, Jerusalem and Mecca are known for their religious affiliations. These associations create cities with characteristics that can be marketed for tourists, often symbolized by a single image such as the Eiffel tower. Most often, that single image is not really appropriate and rather too simplistic for the complex web of activity that forms a city, though it may be a starting point for understanding the city as a region. Most cities are made up of pockets or districts of activity that also take on particular visual characteristics.

At the local level, a neighborhood can be observed as a street, a school, a beehive and stand of trees. At the regional level the scale increases to include villages, towns, watersheds, deserts and geological features as vast as the Great Lakes of North America. A region is usually defined as much by natural phenomena as by political events. At the national and international levels political and ethnic divisions may be more apparent than natural ones. A well-balanced nation will be anthropocentric—people oriented— and biocentric—nature oriented. A region (if well-balanced) will be concerned with ANTHROPOCEN-TRISM and BIOCENTRISM. An easier term that embraces both is SOCIAL ECOLOGY, in which the parts of the whole are mutually beneficial and complementary.

How has a creative person brought these various levels together into a social ecology? John Makepeace of Dorset, England, offers an illustrious example. Makepeace has organized production by highly skilled makers of the furniture he designs. Parallel to this is The School for Craftsman in Wood, which he founded and directs. This part of Makepeace's project is set up in Parnham House, whose architecture dates back to the 12th century. In the forest nearby is Hooke Park College, housed since 1989 in experimental architecture built using the forest thinnings. Pure and applied research within architecture, design, art, and making has spawned a new awareness and new levels of

> We must learn to dissolve our past conceptions of (historical) time based in the philosophical and cultural traditions of the "discoverers," which have marred our true sense of geographic and cultural identity, and seek to understand that culture is a flexible system of eco-independent interrelations.
>
> ✎
>
> JOHN K. GRANDE
> INTERTWINING: LANDSCAPE, TECHNOLOGY, ISSUES, ARTISTS

> We still perceive nature as a subject somehow distinct from human culture. We tend to miss the point that everything that surrounds us, including ourselves, derives from nature, however radically transformed the products, life forms, architectures, topographies and landscapes might be.
>
> ✧
>
> JOHN K. GRANDE
> INTERTWINING: LANDSCAPE, TECHNOLOGY,
> ISSUES, ARTISTS

production as people move on from Parnham to other communities. The Makepeace program is based in semiotics and in the study of our relationship to the living tree and the ecology of the forest as sustainable resource. The program becomes international through the people that travel to the site, study within the schools, and attend special seminars. The furniture designed under Makepeace's personal supervision is widely collected and can be seen in The Art Institute of Chicago and the Victoria and Albert Museum. The cultural mix, semiotic flux, and thorough concern for quality and permanence are what make the program strikingly regional, yet cosmopolitan and internationally relevant.

The relationship between two countries may be close because of regional similarities and concerns. Maritime fishers and prairie farmers will obviously connect along natural borders rather more readily than along political ones. In countries as big and diverse as Canada, the United States, and Australia, immense and complex geography makes it

essential to examine appearance within the manageable scale of a region.

Objects appear outside us and even detached from us—this seems especially true when we travel. The objects and images in our home region are part of us, rich in meaning and alive in our experience of place. The principles of appearance for a region—that is, its physical character, stories of place, how we are organized, and the phenomena of site—will often apply at the national level, but the guiding stories and images have to embrace a greater diversity. Diversity in itself affects the ideas of appearance. The kite shows four essential ingredients for a region. What makes one region different from another? Identity begins with ORIGINS, the original aspect of a place. The obvious appearance stems from the IMAGES and STORIES that we see and hear associated with a region. How are the phenomena of place and the stories we tell one another organized? How are MATERIALS and TOOLS used to create the art, artifacts and architecture of a place?

**Elmstead Market,
Essex, UK**
1996

Mud on paper
30 x 22"
Jason Gathorne-Hardy
Essex, UK

Jason Gathorne-Hardy works
with a natural material, mud.
Cave paintings used mud; so does
the space shuttle with ceramic
tiles on its nose cone. Gathorne-
Hardy was educated as a scientist
but later became a painter. He has
said, *"If my work can be reduced to
a simple aim, it is to translate the
energy of the land into paintings
for other people to see... painting is
the coming together of being in a
place at a time and feeling
relaxed. Painting there is like an
imprint of the time and place."*

Working with the materials, forms
and energies of a place will
inevitably resonate within the
community, if the community has
an appreciation for the original, in
this case their landscape and
natural surroundings.

ORIGIN AND ORIGINAL

A place is made up from natural phenomena, cultural objects, and
environments. What originated the place? Was it the eruption of the
earth's surface to form mountains, or the laying down of limestone at
the bottom of a sea? A succession of plants and animals moved into the
region, inhabiting it and cohabiting in particular and unique
arrangements. Early people congregated at sites where there was
abundant fish life, stone formations for making tools and projectile
points, or a particular landform that engendered a sense of safety or
spirituality. Because of human habitation some animals will move out
as others move in to live on the fringe of the site or to become tame and
live in the same dwellings as the people. Today, the place for wildlife to
live, the levels of material production, and the methods used to organize
ourselves all have changed dramatically. Even so, communities continue
to relate to the resources of the region. Objects made and subjects
presented will come from the materials and the stories of the region.

Scientists, in particular the biologist or geologist, will show the
communities of a region how the appearance of place has changed
over time, due to natural events or human interaction, or both.
Sometimes the environment looks right, but on closer inspection and
analysis we learn that it is out of balance: too many chemicals run
into the river, the deer breed too rapidly for the available habitat,
raiding the glacial moraine for gravel has altered the natural
geography and appearance of place. There are sites of special

> Vernacular is used to describe the
> common voice. The vernacular is the
> familiar: in the good judgment of the
> population it is a preferred way of saying,
> doing or making something.
>
>

Bog Heap with Two Alders
1995

Juncas & Pond Muck
4' x 10' x 6'
Susan Englebry
Bolinas, California, USA

There is nothing quite like a good compost heap if you enjoy gardening and what does that have to do with any of the disciplines outside horticulture? Susan Englebry talks about how her work links with her current involvement with restorative land management practices:

"The land where I work and study brought me back to my uneducated art days. Its pace, requirements and rewards are the same. Aspects of mythic cause and effect are evident in land as they were in those early art days. They are present in the soils, in the movement of water and in the acorn harvest. They can be tasted in honey taken from hives during a certain month in summer. They blend the bouquet of an entire watershed when all debris from the previous season begins to ferment with the rains.

"My function is to do the bidding of grand and respectable unknowns, and be willing to live with the unknown results. I am urged to assume what reasonable individuals would consider outrageous. The strongest assumption is that what calls me to reverence will prosper."

Although Bog Heap with Two Alders is contemporary it is also reminiscent of the childhood game of serving imaginary meals with *"sticks and bits of bark and leaves and piles of soil for invisible and actual dinner guests... So it occurred to me that this is what I am still getting at, but it is all just taking longer these days, as it comes through two different modes. Through one, it is the management of soils to end up with a comestible; in the other, in art, it is by serving of the components of soil as a sacrament."*

scientific interest that need to be maintained for their biodiversity and geological features. These are original places that tell the story of the world. Ultimately any place has a story that can be told through the imagination of the artist.

Television has had a devastating influence on some people. No longer do they see themselves. Instead, they ape the behaviors originating in film centers and they take on the cynicism of those markets. Television potentially boils original stories with all their subtle richness and diversity into a universal solution that can be readily understood by a very average intelligence from almost any culture—the lowest common denominator. At the same time television and movies sometimes do present a simple story well told that can be appreciated by many people. If anything were all bad we tend to not continue doing it. Survival demands we not be 100% stupid.

Pervasive mass media makes it more difficult to see and create our own stories. In a small community, stories emerge easily through the chatter of the day. Capturing the original stories, bracketing them, binding and building them into lasting memories, is rather more complex for the cultural worker in the small community. Nevertheless this activity is critical because it is only in the original stories of a community of shared experiences that the self-image of individuals can grow.

STORIES AND IMAGES

Around the gathering sites, whether at the family dining table, the theater, city council meetings, or the water cooler in the office, stories are told. These **STORIES** are about the **PHENOMENA OF PLACE** and the activities of the region. Images are evoked that illustrate, explain, and vivify the events of our lives, and those of the people from the region. Memories are captured in objects and some of these objects are so powerful in telling the story, they lodge in the imagination of the community. Two images occur: first, a painting by Tom Thomson, a local hero to my region and to many in Canada. The painting is called *The West Wind* and shows a lone tree blown in the wind against a background of whitecaps on a lake, a silhouette of richly dark hills, and

Grape Basket for Growers
1992

Natural Australian materials
57 x 59cm
Pat Dale
Leongatha, Victoria, Australia

Everything is made from nature and some things are closer to their origins than others. Making from these "natural" or "original" materials of a region will inevitably create characteristic forms and colors that are particular to place. In manufacturing, materials are processed to become something else—fiberboard, paper,

Similarity, consistency, and dependability are the demands of world markets and mass production. These products create a demand for bland conformity of appearance.

Pat Dale's Grape Basket for Growers is the antithesis to conformity of material and production. Nature is selectively collected for its

woven to form the basket. The hairy, tough roughness and the shiny, smooth surfaces are particular to the Australian bush. The vine of the handle connects the idea of the basket back to the vineyards of Australia. In a time of industrial agriculture, Grape Basket for Growers is a symbolic form. It is nostalgic for that hot dusty day when, as the sun set it was perfect

wildly colorful sky. It is an icon of the Canadian wilderness. The second image is a drawing of trees by Emily Carr, who painted the great forests of British Columbia. Her image acts as an icon of the scale of the country and the diversity of the land. Woven into these two images is the story of the artists' lives and the regions in which they lived and created their projects. This past summer our regional theater performed a play about Tom Thomson's life, called *Colors in the Storm*.

The images of a place signify a relationship not only for the signifier (the person who created the work) but also for the signified. Maker, subject, object, and viewer become engaged in a balanced way.

When we think about a region it is often in association with its geography and what the people have made of the land. Modernism and the International style tend to override the VERNACULAR and INDIGENOUS, in its place raising a single voice that cares not for local traditions and the specificity of a location. However, the concept of the GLOBAL VILLAGE simultaneously offers the perception of the macro and the micro in the framework of MODERNITY. At its best, POST MODERNISM is more inclined to see the issues of cultural identity as relationships between communities to resolve and nurture. What can be better than telling the stories, showing images and objects through an animated exchange between international communities in a spirit of concerned interest for the physical, emotional, spiritual, and intellectual well-being of others?

> Indigenous refers to who and what belongs to a particular site. It is native to or original to a place.
> ↺

ORGANIZATION

The plasticity of culture unfolds, folds, moulds, stretches, and shapes with every new nuance. The land is affected and the balance changes. Thousand-year-old trees are cut down and the habitat changes. These familiar images become memories, fading and then replaced by contemporary views of our eroded sense of place. The organization of images subtly shifts and occasionally strikes us harshly as the new reality of an old subject. The creator of the stories and images continually recreates in the light of the new appearance. The stories and images situate our experience in the past, present, and what the future may hold. The method of organization encodes our experience so we can each see and talk about the same experience. Language—whether spoken or visual—unites regions with particular accents evolved from their mutual encounter.

Organizations and institutions act as a collective memory and presenter of our past. Our stories are not entirely an aural account. Every club and association has its files with minutes of meetings, press clippings, membership lists. Rather boring compared to the stories told by the older board member about such-and-such event and its resolution. In the adventures of D. B. Murphy by Richard Thomas and in particular in his mystery novel, *The Lost Tyre Gang*, the sense of place of the characters presents a wonderful view of my region. This fictional account is by no means an official history even though it is solidly based in key facts. Museums and galleries collect and present in a more thorough manner, perhaps, than novelists. But they too are constructing fictions for the cognoscenti, school groups, and tourists. Museums that collect narrowly may exaggerate and indulge a nostalgic memory. Meanwhile the contemporary moment may be retained through the private collector who, in time, passes the collection on to the institution. In these transactions, what gets remembered and who does the remembering? In my local library there are 109 entries for local histories, but only five deal with the arts. Yet, our region is often touted for its keen interest in and support for the arts.

MATERIAL AND METHOD

In the past, before today's highly effective transportation system, environments and places were made from local materials in quite specific ways. In some respects the system of manufacture and transportation has become so effective that our regions begin to look the same. Materials from away are like the spices from another country— exotic because they are unfamiliar. For some, curiosity leads to the exotic becoming a matter of status, affecting the story and implying an image of greater control than merely owning what is local. Other people are quite happy with what they have, they deliberately set out to make using the materials of their region, creating a lively vernacular form that may become an icon for their region. The wood-shingled turrets of the Russian Orthodox church, stone pyramids from Egypt, and the organic adobe forms of Mexican buildings are examples of architecture that have come to symbolize their regions.

Here is another example. In Melbourne, Australia, many homes have cast-iron balustrades that act as a functional decoration. Although not an indigenous material or form, they are a familiar sight associated with that place. Melbourne's early settlers set out from Britain in boats that needed ballast for stability. This ballast provided the material for the cast-iron balustrades, while the memory of Britain provided the pattern. The migratory flux of people from one place to another brought with them particular materials and a particular aesthetic that changed the place.

Another less romantic effect of materials on community is the impact of a travelling salesman who sells a particular color or material for the sides of homes. What results is a linear aesthetic running through the countryside that has little to do with its regional character. This kind of activity changes the appearance of a community to reflect the national sales plan of an international company. Today, with the phantasmagoric display of materials at the franchised local merchant, it becomes difficult to build in an indigenous manner. Science and technology offer new materials, or old materials in new forms. Like processed foods, we are a few steps removed from the original. Roads, bridges, and buildings are constructed using the new materials enabled by scientific discovery and engineering prowess. But each of us is a maker constructing our own place, if only by rearranging the interiors of our homes.

When I set out to build my studio in an indigenous manner I found compromises and the inevitable seeping of cultural and material influences. The building is essentially a traditional form based on the Ontario barn but constructed of a less expensive, more modern and weather-tight material and finish than traditional barns. The limestone skimmed from the bedrock to make a basement forms a stony surround and sets the building into its familiar context. Despite my good intentions, the vernacular voice succumbed to the corporations and what they offer at affordable prices. When I was constructing the windows I ran short on materials. I had purchased the local white cedar. It was comparable in price to western red cedar, but my local supplier was a 20-minute drive away during a February snowstorm. The difficulty of driving with the car's back window open to accommodate the long boards, plus the price of fuel, was worth more than materials brought from thousands of miles away.

CONCLUSION

There is on occasion an uneasy relationship between the local, regional, national and international. Will one dominate? How will consensus be reached? History, even the 20th century, is steeped in imperialism and colonialism. How we live together and create the environment will always be a fundamental concern. The new internationalism is very different from the International style—a style that homogenized our city centers into corporate visions of similarity, efficiency, and dominance. The new internationalism explores the relationship of centers to the periphery, and values those activities where difference, genuine interest, and mutuality are the benchmarks of interaction. The only exchange may be secular—a discourse on the technologies of interaction.

Inevitably there will be appropriation and assimilation. A region cannot live in total isolation if it wants any of the benefits that the 20th century has provided. Through science, the technology of computers and the Internet connects the regions in entirely new ways. A map of the world in 1900 is also very different from today's map. Perhaps no region remains untouched by technological advances. Today it is possible to chat through telephone and the computer with counterparts in other nations while using images and instantly transmitting complex data. You would think this would help us toward a tolerant and just society. In all this flux and change the artist, designer, maker, and scientist still identifies the sense of place, constructing the spaces in which we live in our community and our region.

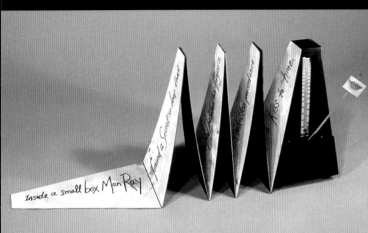

CHAPTER TEN

Critical Methods

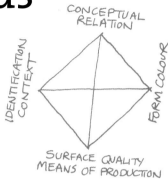

CONCEPTUAL
RELATION

IDENTIFICATION
CONTEXT

FORM COLOUR

SURFACE QUALITY
MEANS OF PRODUCTION

OVERVIEW

Critical methods show how to get inside appearance and how to think about the experience of the work. There are many ways to do this. Some methods are appropriate to makers, critics, scholars, and educators. When these are understood, appearance opens into a rich vocabulary of perceptions and insights about reality.

CRITICAL PERFORMANCE

People have a variety of different responses to the experience and appreciation of a work. The appearance of our environment is out there, detached from us, and yet when it is seen in the eye and mind it is in us. What do we do with appearance as it gently alights in the mind and memory? A simple sequence may include the pleasure of **LOOKING**, **SEEING**, **UNDERSTANDING**, and the sense of **CONNECTION**. Depending on the work and the circumstances, the order and emphasis will swing from one pole to another. The poles may always vary in importance. This dilemma is part of the excitement of the experience.

CONCEPTUAL RELATIONSHIP

FORM AND COLOR

SURFACE QUALITY
MEANS OF PRODUCTION

IDENTIFICATION / CONTEXT

To understand the work it is helpful to understand the context in which the work is presented. An apple cannot be evaluated in the same way as a car. An apple

Stoneware Vase
1992

9-1/2 x 6"
Stoneware
Steve Irvine
Grey County,
Ontario Canada

DESCRIPTION—FORM AND COLOR

The form is circular through one axis and essentially a modified cylinder. A spherical form starts to emerge in the upper body and is echoed in the lower. The curves are fully blown but not like a drawn circle. The object feels gently full, with pressure coming from the inside. The waist band prevents a completely spherical or cylindrical appearance. The lip is consistent with the upper body of the pot and uses large radii to join body to neck. The pebble-like surface of dots recedes from the base while swelling up to a red-brown clay-colored band. The form swells out and back to the vase lip. Another fine brown line contains the outward thrust. These two brown lines contrast an inward tug against an outward thrust. The colors are stone white at the base on a red clay ground, the body is the color of a gray-green lichen with red, purple, and blue shimmering subtly beneath the green. The green glaze is glossy and wet, thickest and most luxurious on the shoulder or top, like moss on a boulder.

SURFACE QUALITIES AND MEANS OF PRODUCTION

The vase is made from clay on a potter's wheel. The surface of the base is textured by a glaze that puddles into dots. A red clay band in the lower center is echoed in the edge of the generous lip. The upper body is smooth and shiny up to the neck and down into the cavernous interior. The bottom of the foot has an off-center pattern like a clamshell or mollusk. Balancing the center of the pattern's energy is a squared mark with the letters S I for Steve Irvine, the potter.

CLASSIFICATION

It is a pot for flowers. It does not evoke any particular season and would look as well with fresh spring or summer flowers as dried flowers in the autumn. Some pots only want to be looked at but this pot looks best with a strong bouquet and is very receptive to plants of a broad range of color, scale, and texture. Historically, Irvine places the work as inspired by the Tang Dynasty (618-907 AD) and Sung Dynasty (960-1279 AD). He tells the story of an exceptional experience:

"I was well acquainted with the pottery of the Tang and Sung Dynasties before visiting the collector's home. I had studied the fine collection at the Royal Ontario Museum many times. What made my visits to the collector's home so special was that I could touch and feel the weight of the pieces. Most of the pieces in use at the house were vases of flowers, forsythia, and wide bowls of forced bulbs. A few small bowls may have held candies etc. but I don't recall eating any meals off the old pieces. Nonetheless, the direct contact did affect me deeply. Seeing a 1000-year-old thumb print on the foot of a bowl and putting my thumb on the same spot and imagining the bowl being glazed gave me a profound sense of continuity across time and cultures."

CONCEPTUAL INTERPRETATION

It is a pot that can be just looked at. I have developed a relationship to the pot through its form and surface quality. I may well be projecting an idea and not what is there or what you see but what follows is the view I hold of the piece. Its form, texture, and color reflect the land in which it was made. The area is referred to as Stoney Keppel. Most beaches on the east side of the Bruce Peninsula are made from water-rounded pebbles and rocks. Often the beach and land meet in a mat of reddish-brown soil, grasses and cedar roots, before rolling into the gently curving countryside. Erratic outcrops of glacially rounded limestone rocks leave beach lines with marooned rocks covered by moss and lichen under a canopy of coniferous and deciduous trees. While not entirely contrived or intentional, the potter has created a piece that responds intuitively to the regional qualities of the land. He has originated an aesthetic experience from his region. It is, for me, a vernacular vase even if there is an influence from China. It is not wildly original but clearly has a feeling of its origins. Sometimes that is a preferred solution—to see cut flowers placed back into a sympathetic setting with a concern for the original.

153

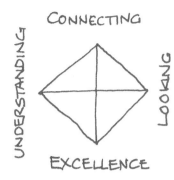

and a painting of an apple cannot be evaluated in the same way either, because they come from entirely different contexts. They can only be compared if a connection can be found that is worth exploring. They have different functions and are made from different materials. The style of painting has interest in relation to other paintings; the apple has interest in relation to other kinds of apple. The subject is tenuously the same but the "functions" are different.

A discussion of the relationship of the painted apple to the rest of the world might work like this: material determines the kind of technique that forms the apple, and the form of the apple determines the kind of apple to be created. It can work back the other way too. If the subject is the apple then we may choose a green or red apple, large or small. The material and technique follow the demands of the subject and its proposed context. If the maker has a bias toward one discipline then he or she will tend to think of technique, form, subject or their own concerns first, and perhaps will think about the other aspects later.

There is profound danger in rushing to judge a

CONNECTING

    LOOKING / SEEING

EXCELLENCE

    UNDERSTANDING

work. Nothing is quite what it appears on first encounter; on the second encounter one's opinion may well change again. Therefore we will look more closely at how to perform a critique, and this will put us into the right frame of mind to make better judgments about the appearance of things. How can criticism become an effective and mind-expanding experience?

For me, criticism in art school was bittersweet. The objects we had painstakingly developed sat proudly, sloppily, meekly, defiantly, beautifully in the center of a small group of people. Our instructor guided each of us to talk about what we had created and why it was in the form it was. After our individual interpretations we then listened, discussed and argued with our fellow students and the instructor. These were highly charged intellectual and emotional encounters during which we not only developed our own perceptions, but also developed an inkling about the experience of another person. There was no room for those who felt one thing and said another; intellectual dishonesty and mannerisms were ousted in favor of directness, honesty, humor, sharing of insight, and an acceptance of the foolhardy comment when well intentioned. This was the environment in

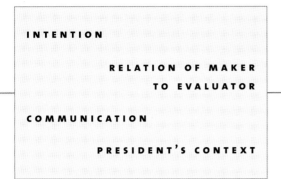

INTENTION

RELATION OF MAKER
TO EVALUATOR

COMMUNICATION

PRESIDENT'S CONTEXT

which I learned most about making, how to see, and more importantly, why make anything at all.

There are some basic ways to improve the critique and the interaction among people. These include:

COMMUNICATIONS METHOD—or the quality of the message. The environment in which the critique takes place will affect how a person receives the message. It is desirable to have a sense of security and trust between the evaluator and the maker. Pertinent means to communicate the ideas include not only words, but also gestures, drawings, photographs, examples, and diagrams. Every critical statement should be made in a spirit of sensitive excitement, as if it is the last observation one will make before being struck dumb. Analogies and comparisons develop into different ways of viewing the work, opening a broader range of possibilities.

RELATIONSHIP OF THE EVALUATOR TO THE MAKER—and the ability to send and receive messages. It is more effective to describe than to judge. Facts, not hunches, will share pointed information on the topic. Being specific, not general, maintains the target. It is best to give information or advice when it is requested, not to impose it because we think the other person needs

it. The critique is only useful if the maker can change from his or her current position; if one's position is unchangeable, suggestions only generate frustration. Feedback should be shared now when it is needed, not later when it is too late.

INTENTION OF THE MAKER—that is, why it was made, what might be changed, and does it lead to further ideas? A concise written statement by the maker can help to focus on what was being attempted. It is easier to talk about a body of work or a series of projects concerned with the same basic concept. When only one object is presented, the maker is apt to be protective. With several works comparison becomes easier, and analysis becomes deeper and richer.

PRECEDENTS AND CONTEXT—what has gone before can act as a touchstone or benchmark for the experience. From our experience we abstract what we think to be true or pertinent to us. These abstractions become signs fixed on the map of experience. When we reach some new territory, we check our map to see if we have been here before. What interests me in this metaphor is that I can show you my map but you cannot experience my experience. Presented with the same external

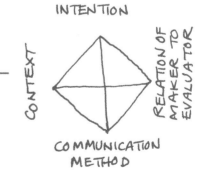

N. Gravity 2
1997

Oil and enamel paint on
cast bronze
160 x 240 x 150cm
Anthea Williams
Boolarra, Victoria, Australia

DESCRIPTION OF THE FORM AND COLOR
From two leaningcircles an agitated line cantilevers out and presents a small square. Although extended beyond the similar configuration of the base, the line appears to be coiled and ready to spring out to its full extent, perhaps three times its present length. The active character of the arm contrasts with the calm circular elements and the cool-blue square plate. The red and yellow colors emphasize the agitated line. Painted sporadically and brightly, the total form is highly active.

THE MEANS OF PRODUCTION
Cast in bronze and painted, the piece is unique. Although potentially reproducible, it is made from a burn-out process whereby the molten bronze is poured into a mould surrounding the original form. When the mould is broken away, the original form appears transmuted into the hard bronze metal.

IDENTIFICATION AND CLASSIFICATION
This is clearly the work of a sculptor who is also interested in drawing, collage, and assemblage. Its strongest roots will be found in the sculpture of David Smith, Anthony Caro, and Nancy Graves, and there are references to Jackson Pollock and Cy Twombly. Each of these artists at some point combined found or manufactured elements and assembled them into their own configurations and constructions. In N. Gravity 2 the geometry to the circles and square contrasts with the active lines. Anthea Williams says, *"My sculpture is an interplay between the found object and made form. Between the, common icons and abstract forms, there is a reconciliation creating a new and unified set of relationships."* In this piece there is a latent built-up energy of a snake about to strike, or of one element passing through or springing from another. The nature of the line is hurriedly drawn, a line that captures the energy of the arm that made the mark.

CONCEPTUAL RELATIONSHIP —INTERPRETATION
The circles are like the shells of crustaceans, the eggs of a crocodile, or the birth of a cold, blue square that projects into space. But these are projections I put onto the work and they may be irrelevant. Projecting one's own view must be done with extreme caution. It is easy to fall into colonizing the work with one's own bias and thus to be careless in investigating the truth. Can we intellectually meet the artist in the work and agree to a meaning? More probably, the work refers to the abstract pursuits of the artist in developing forms that hint at phenomena, rather than to the specifics of any one perception. The viewer is obliged to feel the form, rather than to label the construction. While there are three primary elements—line, circle, square—the work seems to present the relationship between and interaction of spontaneity and emotion. When I contemplate the work it gives me the sensation of drawing rapidly on paper with that action translated into the third dimension: a moment of movement captured in a human eternity. The aesthetics of the sketch, and the feeling of closeness to the maker's mark, captures the gestures of life. Although the sculpture is ambiguous, which is a satisfactory conceptual relationship, it does formally create what Williams calls "...a new unified set of relationships."

variables, we can each only have our own inner experience. Apart from personal experience there is the sum total of society's experience. Measuring the work against that is complex and awesome, but ultimately it is what everyone has to do.

Analysis in the critique is easier said than done. It is all so extremely complex and woven into one aesthetic cloth. By pulling it apart one stitch at a time, we may learn about stitching, but not about the aesthetic experience the cloth gives us.

Thus far this discussion of critique has been about the relationship of the maker to the evaluator, but many of the same observations apply to self-criticism. Perhaps that is where criticism should start—in developing the skills to look at one's own work. In self-criticism I have found it helpful to sleep on the problem, put it away for an extended period of time, look at it in a mirror, or change the quality of light on the subject. Stand

well back from it, turn it upside down or sideways, take a photograph, and so on. Find other ways to look. If all these fail to reveal a useful perspective, then seek help from others. The danger of self-criticism is that it can become mental flagellation, self-deprecation, perfectionist slaughter. It can result in the inability to laugh at oneself or to penetrate beneath the fear of failure. The most difficult critique is self-criticism, yet it must be done, or else the maker will become the instrument of the critic and may fail to develop an inner sense of what is right and true.

CRITICAL DISCIPLINES

Each discipline approaches critiques of the work from its own point of view. The four main disciplines are **JOURNALISM, SCHOLARSHIP, PEDAGOGY,** and **POPULAR OPINION**. It is important to expect a review by a journalist to be different from one by a scholar. A school teacher will review the work of a student in quite a different way than the public responding to a new experience. The ability to criticize well is based on breadth of experiences, knowledge of the field, willingness to try new things, and the ability to feel and interrogate, or to explore along with the person who created the work.

SELF EVALUATION

SCHOLARLY ANALYSIS

PEDAGOGICAL DISCUSSION

JOURNALISTIC DESCRIPTION

SELF EVALUATION

PEDAGOGICAL DISCUSSION

JOURNALISTIC DESCRIPTION

SCHOLARLY ANALYSIS

JOURNALISTIC DESCRIPTION

Most people are informed by journalists' reporting of events in which new work is presented to the public. This is news and as such it should focus on fact and description, rather than on opinion. However, opinion is impossible to keep out of journalism. The decision to cover this exhibition or that one, and such seemingly minor factors as whether the reviewer is a man or a woman, can result in tremendous differences in presentation and content by the magazine or newspaper. The slant of the commentary also will depend on the kind of newspaper it is. The populist newspaper, bent on quantity of readers, will be assertive and short on analysis, skimming the essence of the controversy or subject. A magazine can afford a longer analysis to make a point or develop a thesis.

The journalistic style does tend to promote one person or position over another; it develops a critical discourse that may stir the pot of controversy. The party line of one persuasion over another whips up cheerleaders and followers much like an endless game of attention-getting. This is largely done for the market economy rather than

for the search for truth. Taking trendy and fashionable positions can result in the work being denigrated. It is a matter of how far the spirited writing, and jockeying for attention is taken. Certainly readers must retain their own critical faculties, and decide for themselves not only about the work under discussion, but also about the motivations and quality of the writing itself.

It is best to read journalism as news and not let it affect your opinion until you have seen the work yourself and reached your own conclusions. Alas, so much is going on it is impossible to see everything. We often have to rely on the integrity of the reporter as the front line of information delivered with a dash of opinion.

SCHOLARLY ANALYSIS

Criticism by the scholar should reflect the full weight of years of study in a particular field. The scholar's knowledge is as complete as might be found anywhere. Yet scholarly writing may become convoluted, getting in the way of clarity. There is some science I shall never understand, many techniques of making that will elude me, and some scholarly writing I will never comprehend. Perhaps that is the nature of specialization. However, the scholar should be able to place the work in the broader context of the society in which the work was made. The ability to analyze, interpret and place a value on the work is central to the scholar's work. The scholar is usually found in an institution surrounded by the research facility, information banks, and the economic security essential to the long-term commitment that scholarship requires. In some ways the academy provides the final voice of reason and

The Garden Building at Woodbridge Lodge, Rendlesham, Suffolk, UK
1995

Hugh Pilkington

Suspend judgment until you have experienced The Garden Building first hand. Perhaps that should be true for every project represented in *Appearance and Reality*. The original will always "tell" you more than an image in a book, magazine, or on a television screen. The advantage of intermediation through the various media is filtration that collects the insights and takes out some of the effort to do a proper evaluation for oneself. A few hard facts can go a long way to dispel mysteries, or to present the relevant mysteries. It is probably impossible, certainly unfair, to pass a definitive judgment from one photograph and a couple of paragraphs. It may be realistic to develop a tentative opinion from the information conveyed through various media. When we do go out for the first-hand encounter we are better prepared than if we knew nothing or approached the work with abject ignorance. A "brochure" does help frame how we should initially approach the work.

The Garden Building at Woodbridge Lodge is presented through just one image—a view from the top of a tree. The view gives us a better idea of the major relationships of the two adjoining buildings and a sense of the plan. The original Georgian Folly and gate house, ca. 1806, has been added to with the garden wall creating the back for the new home. Some of the finishes inside the home are screed-sealed, waxed, and polished. White plastered walls are waxed and polished. Timber is sealed and stained using natural dyes, pigments and oils—no paint.

Our appreciation for the project has to remain essentially conceptual rather than sensory. It is unfortunate because this project may well be exceptional at a sensory level as one passes through the grounds, the Georgian Folly, and a contemporary home that primarily uses materials in their original form. The delight of the relationship of the Folly to the environmentally appropriate home comes through the unexpected juxtaposition of ideological meanings.

In looking at the single image we can only guess at the problems that faced the architect and client. The architect's notes reveal some of the considerations:
    difficult planning problems,
    complex listed-building
        negotiations,
    challenging historical
        setting,
    secret architecture,
    joining old to new,
    environmentally friendly,
    energy efficient,
    low budget,
    great clients.
The list is interesting because it appears primarily as a list of problems but "great clients" can hardly be seen as a problem. It does rather turn our perception toward the excitement of a challenge that had to have been felt by the architect. It is in the process of resolution that some of the interest and pleasure of its appearance must evolve. It is therefore essential not to think of architecture as merely an image but as a series of processes that culminate with a particular form.

A description of a building's appearance is not likely to deliver a purpose or a meaning. Appearance is deceiving, so it is essential to gather the pertinent information on the building's program and to measure the results against the intentions. The Garden Building at Woodbridge Lodge, with its two fundamentally different forms of architecture, makes that point very clear. What does a home, factory, hospital, museum, gallery, or school look like? Either architects are very confused, or they don't begin with generic forms. Architecture has to be conceptualized as a whole and to achieve that there are many questions to ask and much information to collect before pencil can be put to paper in the all-knowing conceptual sketch. In the same spirit, the viewer or critic also must assemble the data in order to assess the work. It is of course possible to make great-looking buildings that do not work for the participants, but an ugly building is just that—almost forever. From the single image of Woodbridge Lodge I think it is possible to see that the architect and client have created an appearance with a delightful relationship between the environment, the old, and the new.

To evaluate a building, courtesy insists that a request be made for viewing unless it is open to the public. Normally most homes are not open for the rabble of tire-kickers, gawkers, tourists and inquisitors like myself prying into appearance and reality. Having established its availability and purpose, then walk through and around the spaces. Sniff the air, rub the surfaces, listen to the sound of your feet and the echoes in the air. How was the building made? Is this a low cost building made from factory parts, is it handmade from local materials, is it environmentally sensitive, and so on? How do you classify the architecture and identify the important features? Does the project have integrity where all the parts fit together to create a harmonious whole while respecting difference?

> A fool sees not the same tree
> that a wise man sees.
>
> BLAKE

sound judgment: the place where the artist's story becomes tied into the fabric of the culture. If that sounds too definitive, it is important to note that the definitive scholarly work may be challenged or reopened years later. New ideas emerge. A new appreciation develops in which older works demand reappraisal.

PEDAGOGICAL DISCUSSION

Teachers have a particularly difficult role to play. They have to be aware of the art of the day, the art of the past, the development of the student and, not to forget, their own work as well. Most of this has to be discussed with the student in the context of what the student wants to learn. In the past the student apprenticed to the master and learned his skills. Sometimes the student becomes radical from the master's point of view, growing away physically and mentally to form his or her own particular perception of the discipline and subject. Today, unfortunately, the student, and perhaps society as well, expects to be radical immediately, with pretty clear instruction on how to make a living and to gain some notoriety. And the instructor had better help the student get there forthwith. Inevitably this leads to the pedagogical discussion of ways and means of unravelling the experience.

Important in the pedagogical discussion is the need to develop the ability of the student toward independence, along with the critical ability to recognize his or her own work. To do this it is necessary to take criticism from a variety of people and learn to filter what is appropriate for one's own direction. Students must learn to evaluate other people's work in relation to their own work, and finally to evaluate independently what is happening in their own work. The teacher must guide the students from where they are to where they want to go, without necessarily giving them direct answers. When should some knowledge be offered? When should some know-how be demonstrated? How should the experience of know-what-to-do be demonstrated? What knowledge is essential to complete the assignment?

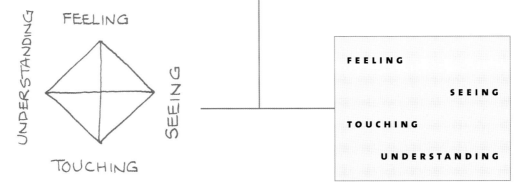

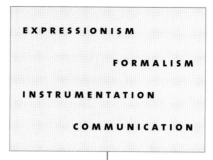

EXPRESSIONISM

FORMALISM

INSTRUMENTATION

COMMUNICATION

POPULAR OPINION

Popular opinion is at best the vernacular voice. It is the steady commentary based in trial and error. At worst, it is over-reaction based in fear of the new. Popular opinion reaction can be the last thing you would have expected to become a problem. Sometimes it makes perfectly good sense and at other times it appears to be the height of the irrational.

The vernacular voice reflects the local wisdom that holds things back and allows a culture to grow within the context of society and the environment. It is the least exciting way of thinking about human experience. However, should the vernacular voice

become criminal it loses its solid foundation and also loses its value. The radical voice becomes the voice of un-common sense.

The majority can have the effect of restraining the creative energy of the few who have exceptional insight. While everybody has the potential to be creative, only occasionally will the majority have the will to be collectively innovative. It is a great culture that can maintain checks and balances among the vernacular voice, teams and partnerships, and the creative genius. These tend to split apart and form their own cultures within society, invariably ending in confrontation that leads nowhere. The metropolitan center can absorb differences more readily than the small center, where greater levels of cooperation are required in order to have anything happen.

CRITICAL MEANS

We need to agree on basic means for assessing the work. There are benchmarks or signposts that have a structure based in the four disciplines. Often the two major tools of reference are form and content. A work is measured by its form first, and its content second, or vice-versa. This oppositional view does start the

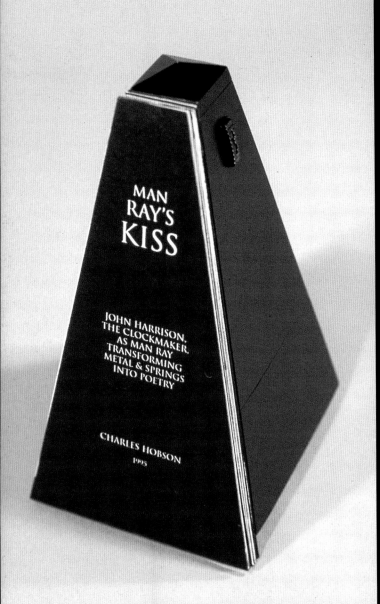

MAN
RAY'S
KISS

JOHN HARRISON,
THE CLOCKMAKER,
AS MAN RAY
TRANSFORMING
METAL & SPRINGS
INTO POETRY

CHARLES HOBSON
1995

Man Ray's Kiss
1995

Metronome book
w/ monotype
9.5 x 5 x 5"
Charles Hobson
San Francisco, California,
USA

Charles Hobson's program Clouds and Dreams: Longitude & Surrealism and his projects such as Man Ray's Kiss are all knowledge-based. The sensory aspect of each project draws the viewer into the intrinsic enigma of the piece. The projects require a knowledge of history that links the 18th century English navigators and the early 20th century avant-garde—in particular the Surrealists. This is presented through the text that accompanies each project and the larger program. Hobson presents intricate, difficult questions presents

through objects, subject, image, and text. A full appreciation of each project is incomplete without a commitment of time to read his text and ponder the enigma of the objects. Even then it is probably necessary to look further at other sources to see more fully the juxtaposition of people and personalities involved. The work is rich in intellectual subtleties and requires a particular inquiring attitude to follow through the process of critical examination. In an introductory statement titled Clouds and Dreams, Charles Hobson writes: *"In 1707, a fleet of four English warships was sailing home from Gibralter under the command of Admiral Sir Clowdisley Shovell. In a thick fog his navigator miscalcula-ted their longitude. Instead of entering the English Channel the fleet ran aground on Scilly Rocks, 200 miles to the west. All four ships and the 2,000 men aboard were lost. In response to the tragedy Parliament passed the Longitude Act, offering a huge prize (nearly $12 million in today's value) to anyone who could provide a reliable way to calculate longi-tude at sea. A cacophony of voices sounded in attempted answer.*

"In 1914 a calamitous and ghastly war devastated Europe. In its ashes the prevailing cultural values and patterns of thought were thrown into question. In 1923, drawing on these questions and new concepts that ranged from Freudian analysis to experimental French poetry, a group of writers and artists gathered in Paris seeking to reclaim the power of the imagination and formulated

an approach they called Surrealism.

"What could possibly link the Surrealists and those who sought the Longitude Prize 200 years earlier? Perhaps it is that each endeavor was triggered by misfortune and calamity. Or is it that each group's pursuits held parallels in how the human mind formulates questions and poses answers?

"Each was dealing with a question of how human beings make their way in the world. In the 1700s, the seekers of the Longitude Prize were looking for a missing coordinate—longitude—to go with something they already knew—latitude. In the 1920s the Surrealists were looking for ways to plumb the imagination and the unconscious to provide an additional coordinate to go with reason and the intellect.

"And so I have arrived at clouds and dreams as metaphors for the parallels between such disparate researches. Clouds filled the sky of the 18th century sailors and the paintings of many of the Surrealist artists. They stand for the imagination and dreams the Surrealists searched, and for the vastness of the world the Prize seekers were attempting to gird with longitude."

On Man Ray's Kiss, Charles Hobson writes: *"Inside a small box Man Ray found a secret so deep that he had no way to keep it. It seeped between his fingers and ran out his eyes with its relentless persistence. Inside his small box light gave a kiss to time and captured the movement of dreams, the shape of imagination."*

> Whenever I have confronted that which was unfamiliar to me I constantly sought neither to praise or condemn, but only to understand.
>
> ∽
> SPINOZA

critical comments unfortunately come from a misconception about the conception, or a narrowly honed position that lacks the breadth of human experience necessary for reading the greater implications of the work.

discussion but it soon falters. There is a rush to judgment because the viewer has attempted to project his or her own patterns of appreciation, instead of receiving what the object transmits and thereby discovering what has been presented.

The four main approaches may be framed as:

WHAT DOES IT EXPRESS?

WHAT IS IT TELLING US?

HOW IS IT USED?

WHAT DOES IT LOOK LIKE?

Sometimes all four questions will be found in one work but usually there is a preference and an emphasis. The work may have been made from a singular point of view, it may combine two of the questions equally. Similarly, some people will evaluate the work from a single perspective. They only care about whether it is beautiful, for example. That approach may succeed if the object was also created from a single point of view. But beauty is an idea that varies enormously from one culture to the next, and finally it is impossible to define. Many

WHAT DOES IT EXPRESS?

EXPRESSIVENESS is concerned with how well, how forcefully, how wittily, or how courageously the idea is presented. It looks for conviction. The art of the "primitive," the child, or the psychotic is not about careful design or accurate communication. It is galvanized with passion and conviction springing from the moment of experience.

The preconscious experience of the artist wells up to let us know what is true. There is an emotional fervor that demands exaggeration and extremes. It is not a controlled world, perfect and beautiful; rather, it tells it like it is. Relevance, intensity, validity, and originality are the tools of expression. Expressiveness will judge the work with these tools.

WHAT IS IT TELLING US?

COMMUNICATION is a two-way process between communicator and receiver. The perceptual psychologist is interested in following as exactly as possible how and why this works. The fidelity of experience, the precise nature of what is being sent and how it is being received, is critical. The aesthetic experience is of interest only because it influences the message. Beauty is truth, truth is fact, and fact is physiology first and psychology second. Can the experience be measured and what does that measurement mean?

HOW IS IT USED?

INSTRUMENTALISM looks at work from the point of view of usefulness. Does it advance political, social, religious, or economic ends? Advertising uses ideas and images to sell products. Generally there is little regard for content so long as the ad sells more product. Religious imagery will evoke pathos, awe, and fear to bring the people to worship. The sexual nature of many advertisements harnesses one of the most powerful motors of the human experience into the service of selling.

The visual arts have always been used by the ruling elite or the democratically appointed to project their message into the minds of society. Some artists will withdraw entirely from any association with power. They are the sole purveyors of ideas, until the ideas meet the market economy. Some artists have created impermanent works which are uncollectable, in a site of their choice where the only evidence is photographic representation. Today the artist stands, more often than not, alone with the choice of materials, forms and content. But not all artists. Graphic designers and product designers create impressive solutions for the market economy. Architects and planners create grand schemes for new towns. The history of art, craft / technology, design, and science is filled with the uneasy relationship among creator, collector, and public. Any human production has implications beyond that of mere desire, and the viewer better pay attention to the motivations of the "originator."

WHAT DOES IT LOOK LIKE?

FORMALISM is concerned with the appearance of the work ahead of any meaning. It is the form that is significant and it determines where enjoyment is to be found. The style, age, political, and social aspects of the work are evaluated through the juxtaposition of form, color, material, and their underlying organization. Within this organization the key principle is for unity in variety. How are all the elements reconciled? Bernard Berenson used the idea of aesthetic value as being life-enhancing: it makes you feel good, regardless of the subject matter. "Good" work in this context should be seen as that which strengthens, invigorates, and electrifies the viewer.

All work communicates through ideal forms which are are generally agreed among sensitive, intelligent people. It is a universalizing ideal that all people, regardless of orientation and context, can appreciate the aesthetic. This implies that the life-enhancing feelings generated by good work are physiological and therefore experienced through the nervous and glandular systems of the body. The formalist tries to see what makes a design work. The artist wants to know what to do to the form to

WHAT DOES IT EXPRESS
WHAT IS IT TELLING US
WHAT DOES IT LOOK LIKE
HOW IS IT USED

make it work. Focusing on form is not a bad idea because it is very difficult to get everybody to agree on anything else.

CRITICAL PROCESS

The introduction of this section established the parameters of sensory seeing and critical seeing, followed by the tension between form and content. In these concluding remarks to Critical Methods, we will benefit by looking beyond dualistic oppositions toward a more inclusive, egalitarian, and progressive inquiry.

The model shows the now-familiar arrangement of four quadrants. Anything created must pass through one of these territories before a well-rounded relationship can be established. The arrows suggest two different starting points that each can lead through the same material before settling on what is our relationship to the work. In considering any project, we start by knowing something about it, having knowledge, having know-how, and knowing what the project might be for. In science these relationships would start with PERCEPTION, RECOGNITION, DISCRIMINATION, and INTERPRETATION. The best way to reveal the project is to not rush to judge or interpret the work, but to go through the critical process in an orderly manner. A description of the form is probably the best place to start. This has a way of slowing down the process, enabling the viewer to see in a more open manner, rather than merely applying a quick label. Description of form may be followed closely by description of the material and its surface qualities, and of how it was put together. Next comes the identification and classification of what

is the context of the project, and what the object is for. Is it primarily an object to be enjoyed on the sensory level or does it present a subject about which we need to think? SUBJECT, CONTEXT, OBJECT, and SELF each must be recognized within the work. What takes precedence, or what is at issue in the project? It is necessary to interpret what was intended by the project. Finally, we can develop a conceptual relationship to the project. The project is a construct or concept of the imagination, and we have to decide how it fits with what we believe to be true, appropriate, and relevant. This is our judgment of the project. It is based on our experience, and on our understanding of the appearance of reality.

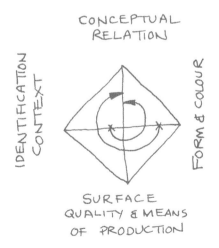

CONCEPTUAL RELATION

IDENTIFICATION CONTEXT

FORM & COLOUR

SURFACE QUALITY & MEANS OF PRODUCTION

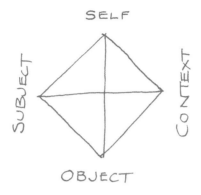

Once more, it is part of the professional skill of a research worker to balance, or oscillate, between faith and scepticism as he threads his way to true understanding. If he remains critical and disbelieving, he may reject an important new insight; if he swallows credulously every fantastic proposal, he will build no more than a theoretical house of cards.

JOHN ZIMAN

Bibliography

This reading list is organized by chapters, and alphabetically within each chapter. Not all titles mesh perfectly with the contents in each chapter but they are timely to read in the sequence of study.

INTRODUCTION

Rudolf Arnheim, *Art and Visual Perception: A Psychology of the Creative Eye, Faber and Faber,* London 1960

R.L.Gregory, *Eye and Brain: The Psychology of Seeing,* Weidenfeld and Nicolson, London 1966-1977

George Kubler, *The Shape of Time: Remarks on the History of Things,* Yale University Press, New Haven, 1962

John Ziman, *Reliable Knowledge: An Exploration of the Grounds for Belief in Science,* Cambridge University Press, Cambridge 1978

E.H. Gombrich, *Art and Illusion,* Phaidon Press, London 1960

1. VISUAL CONTRASTS AND ELEMENTS

Ronald G. Carraher & Jacqueline B. Thurston, *Optical Illusions and the Visual Arts,* Reinhold Publishing Corp., New York 1966

Calvin Harlan, *Vision and Invention: A Course in Art Fundamentals,* Prentice-Hall Inc., Englwood Cliffs, New Jersey 1970

Wassily Kandinsky, *Point and Line to Plane,* Dover 1979 (originally published 1926)

Paul Klee, *Pedagogical Sketchbook,* Faber and Faber, London 1953

Arthur Stern, *How to see Color and Paint It,* Watson Guptill, New York 1984

Lynda Weinman & Bruce Heavin, *Coloring Web Graphics: The Definitive Resource for Color on the Web,* New Riders Publishing, Indianapolis 1996

2. COMPOSITION

Johannes Itten, *Itten: The Elements of Color, Design and Form,* Van Nostrand Reinhold, New York 1970 – 1963

Manfred Maier, *Basic Principles of Design, Van Nostrand Reinhold,* 1977

Wucius Wong, *Principles of Two-Dimensional Design,* Van Nostrand Reinhold, New York 1972

Wucius Wong, *Principles of Three-Dimensional Design,* Van Nostrand Reinhold, New York 1977

Wucius Wong, *Visual Design on the Computer,* Design·Books, New York 1994

3. EXPRESSION

Gaston Bachelard, *The Poetics of Space,* Beacon Press, Boston 1969

Daniel Marcus Mendelowitz, *Mendelowitz's Guide to Drawing,* Holt, Rinehart and Winston, New York 1976

Mike Samuels and Nancy Samuels, *Seeing with the Mind's Eye, The History, Techniques and Uses of Visualization,* Random House Inc. New York 1975

4. PATTERN

Krome Barratt, *Logic & Design in Art, Science & Mathmatics,* The Herbert Press, London 1980

Istvan Hargittai & Magdolna Hargittai, *Symmetry: A Unifying Concept*

Pat Murphy, *By Nature's Design,* Chronicle Books, San Francisco 1993

Michael McGuire, *An Eye for Fractals: A Graphic and Photographic Essay,* Addison-Wesley Publishing Company, Redwood City 1991

Peter S. Stevens, *Patterns in Nature,* Atlantic-Little Brown Books, Boston 1974

Theodor Schwenk, *Sensitive Chaos: The Creation of Flowing Forms in Water and Air,* Rudolf Steiner Press, London 1965

5. TRANSFORMATION

Mike Samuels, MD & Nancy Samuels, *Seeing With the Mind's Eye: The History, Techniques and Uses of Visualization,* Random House Inc. New York 1975

Koberg/Bagnell, *The Universal Traveler: A Soft-Systems Guide to Creativity, Problem Solving and the Process of Reaching Goals,* William Kaufman Inc. 1974

Lewis Hyde, *The Gift: Imagination and the Erotic Life of Property,* Random House, New York, 1979

Vello Hubel and Diedra B. Lussow, *Focus on Designing,* Mc Graw-Hill Ryerson Limited, Toronto 1984

Robert McKim, *Experiences in Visual Thinking,* Books/Cole, Monterey 1972

Clement Mok, *Designing Business: Multiple Media, Multiple Discipline,* Adobe Press, San Jose 1996

Nicholas Roukes, *Design Synectics: Stimulating Creativity in Design,* Davis Publications, Worcester MA, 1988

6. SELF AND OTHER

Carol Adams & Rae Laurikietis, *The Gender Trap — Message and Images,* Virago, London 1976

John Berger, *Ways of Seeing,* Penguin 1972

Johannes Fabian,*Time and the Other: How Anthropology Makes Its Object,* Columbia University Press, New York 1983

A.L.Rees & F.Borzello, (ed) *The New Art History,* Camden Press, London 1986

7. COMMUNICATION

Marshall McLuhan, *Understanding Media:The Extensions of Man,* New American Library, New York 1964

John Fiske, *Introduction to Communication Studies,* Routledge, London 1990

E.H. Gombrich, *Art and Illusion: A Study in the Psychology of Pictorial Representation,* Princeton University Press, Princeton 1960

E.H. Gombrich, *The Image & the Eye: Further studies in the Psychology of Pictorial Representation,* Phaidon Press, London 1982

Ray Kristof & Amy Satran, *Interactivity by Design: Creating and Communicating with New Media,* Adobe Press, Mountain View CA 1995

8. COMMUNITY

Christopher Alexander, Sara Ishikana, Murray Silverstein, *A Pattern Language: Towns, Buildings, Construction,* Oxford University Press, New York 1977

Suzi Gablik, *Conversations Before the End of Time: Dialogues on Art,Life & Spiritual Renewal with...,* Thames and Hudson, London 1995

Suzi Gablik, *The Reenchantment of Art,* Thames and Hudson, New York 1991

Lucy R. Lippard, *Overlay: Contempory Art and the Art of Prehistory,* Pantheon Books, New York 1983

Edward Lucie-Smith, *Race, Sex, and Gender In Contemporary Art,* Harry N. Abrams, Inc., Publishers, New York 1994

Raymond Williams, *Culture,* Collins Publishing Group, 1981

Robert Theobald, *Reworking Success: New Communities at the Millennium,* New Society Publishers, Gabriola Island BC 1997

9. REGION

Robert Brinkhurst (ed), *Visions: Contemporary Art in Canada - Terrance Heath, A Sense of Place,* Douglas & McIntyre Ltd and the Ontario Education Communications Authority, Vancouver 1983

Jean Fisher (Ed), *Global Visions: Towards a New Internationalism in the Visual Arts,* Kala Press, London 1994

Avril Fox, Robin Murrell, *Green Design: A Guide to the Environmental Impact of Building Materials,* Architecture Design & Technology, London 1989

Mark Francis and Randolf T. Hester Jr. (ed), *The Meaning of Gardens,* The MIT Press Cambridge, MA 1990

Nikolaus Pevsner, *The Englishness of English Art,* Penguin Books, 1956 - 1986

Simon Schama, *Landscape and Memory,* Random House of Canada, Toronto 1995

Martin Warnke, *Political Landscape: The Art History of Nature,* Reaktion Books Ltd., 1994

Anne-Marie Willis, *Illusions of Identity: The Art of Nation,* Hale & Iremonger, Sydney 1993

Alexander Wilson, *The Culture of Nature: North American Landscape from Disney to the Exxon Valdez,* Between the Lines, Toronto 1991

10. CRITICAL METHODS

Edmund Burke Feldman, *Varieties of Visual Experience,* Prentice Hall Inc. New Jersey 1987

Susan Woodford, *Looking at Pictures,* Cambridge University Press, Cambridge 1993

Henry M. Sayre, *Writing about Art* (Second Edition), Prentice Hall Inc., New Jersey 1995

GENERAL TITLES

Kieth Albarn and Jenny Miall Smith, *Diagram: The Instrument of Thought,* Thames and Hudson, London 1977

David Bayles & Ted Orland, *Art & Fear: Observations on the Perils(and Rewards) of Art Making,* Capra Press, Santa Barbara 1993

Alan Bowness, *The Conditions of Success: How the modern Artist Rises to Fame,* Thames and Hudson, London 1989

Whitney Chadwick, *Women, Art, and Society,* Thames and Hudson, London 1990

Eric Fernie, *Art History and its Methods: a Critical Anthology — selection and commentary by Eric Fernie,* Phaidon Press, London 1995

Suzi Gablik, Magritte, *Thames and Hudson,* London 1970

E.H. Gombrich, *The Sense of Order: A Study in the Psychology of Decorative Art,* Cornell University Press, Ithica 1979

John K. Grande, *Balance: Art and Nature,* Black Rose Books, Montreal 1994

Ellen Lupton and J. Abbot Miller ed., *The ABC's of the Bauhaus and Design Theory,* Thames and Hudson, London 1993

David Pye, *The Nature & Aesthetics of Design,* Cambium Press, Bethel CT, 1978

David Pye, *The Nature and Art of Workmanship,* Cambium Press, Bethel, CT 1971

Maurice de Sausmarez, *Basic Design: The Dynamics of Visual Form,* Studio Vista, London, 1964

Paul Zelanski & Mary Pat Fisher, *Colour,* Herbert Press, London, 1988

MAGAZINE TITLES

Jan Butterfield, *Art without Objects: Shaping Light and Space,* Sculpture, Sept/Oct 1993

Gareth Jones, *Eulogy for Mass,* F.A.T.E. Conference

Clare C. Brant, *Native Ethics and Rules of Behavior,* Canadian Journal of Psychiatry, Vol. 35, August 1990

Index

A

Abstraction, formality of, 71, 119–21
Appearance:
  contrasts in, 27–28
  defined, 2–3
  and memory, 10–11, 147–48
Art:
  discipline of, 4
  meaning of, 7–10
Artig, Kit, painting by, 112–13
Artworks Gallery, illustrated, 38–39

B

Baty, David, solar cooker by, 18–19
"Bethesda Cemetery," illustrated, 70
Bicknell, Les, art object by, 42
Blunk, J. B., sculpture by, 108
"Bog Heap with Two Alders,"
    illustrated, 144
Bowls:
  paper, 90
  porcelain, 12
  turned, 50, 72
Boyle, John B., painting by, 138–39
Brewer, Kevin, solar cooker by, 18–19
Brinkhurst, Sue, painting by, 120
Broadley, Stephen, pots by, 46
Bruce Peninsular Health Services,
    illustrated, 28–29
Buildings, illustrated, 28–29, 38–39,
    150, 160–61
Bunnell, Kathie, stained glass by,
    24–25
"Burning Labyrinth," illustrated, 132

C

Campbell, Marilyn, bowl by, 72
"Canadology," illustrated, 138
Carleton–McGillis, Michele, painting
    by, 70
"Caryatids 1&2," illustrated, 60
Ceramics:
  plate, 82

  sculpture, 84
  vase, 150, 152
Clough, Eric, et al., structure
    by, 136
Codes, as delimiting agents, 116–17
Coffee pot, sterling, 48
Color:
  additive, 16–17
  analogous, 45, 67
  complementary, 45, 67
  context of, 39
  mixes of, in the eye, 39
  physics of, 16, 26, 27, 30
  and pointillists, 71
  qualities of, 28–29
  subjectivity and, 63
  subtractive, 16–17
  See also Light.
Communication:
  codes of, 115–16
  defined, 168
  methods of, 113
  modes of, 115–16
Community:
  fit to, 127–28
  nuturing, 135
  personal, 131–33
  physical, 133–34
  political, 131
  responsibilities to, 137
  and self–image, 143
  sense of, 135–37
  social, 133
  types of, 128–29
  See also Location; Region.
Composition:
  closure in, 44
  and color, 45
  depth in, 43–44
  formula for, 59
  implied division in, 44–45
  lines of continuation in, 45
  in pictorial space, 41–43
Comprehension, components of, 5–7
Computers:

  color with, 17, 39
  and creativity, 88–89
  depth with, 43–44
  modeling with, 56
  virtual reality with, 53–55
"Confessional," illustrated, 130
Context, and meaning, 57–58, 107,
    109–11
Conway, Ros, drawing by, 2
Cooker, solar, 18–19
"Craftsmanship," illustrated, 110
Craft–technology, discipline of, 4
Creativity:
  and computers, 88–89
  and paradoxes, 92
  physical, 93
  preconscious, 91
  See also Problem solving.
Crehan, Mary, bowl by, 90
Criticism:
  and intention, 155
  journalistic, 160–61
  methods of, 155, 163–66
  pace of, 154
  pedagogical, 160, 161–62
  popular, 160, 162–63
  progressive, 167–69
  scholarly, 160, 161
  self, 160
  See also Sight.

D

Dale, Pat, basket by, 146
Debosegai, Blake, painting
    by, 122–23
Depth, creating, 43–44
Design, discipline of, 4
Dichotomies, restrictions of, 22
Disciplines:
  codes of, 116–17
  integrated, 5, 7
  named, 4
Diversity, and fragmentation, 101
Dixon, Mark, sculpture by, 68

"Dorothy C," illustrated, 122
Drawing:
    concept, 2
    for knowledge, 109
Dunlop Farrow Inc., building by,
    28–29

E
Edwards:
    Kathleen, structures by, 98–99
    Leann, painting by, 104
"8+", illustrated, 42
"Elmstead Market, Essex, UK,"
    illustrated, 142
Emotion:
    coding, 73
    creation of, 61
Enclosure, qualities of, 59
Englebry, Susan, photograph by, 144
Evelegh, Frances, brochure art by, 110
Expressiveness, as content, 168

F
Fabric, wool, silk, rayon, 86
Feldsott, Kenneth C., painting by, 64
"Fifth Season Cycle Centre,"
    illustrated, 136
Flags, as emblems, 74–75
Form:
    additive vs. subtractive, 57
    in exotic materials, 109
    qualities of, 30–33
    shading, 65–66
    and shape, 37
See also Objects
Formalism, standards of, 167
Forster, Hendrik, coffee pot by, 48
Fractals, defined, 83–85

G
Garden Building at Woodbridge
    Lodge, The, illustrated, 150,
    160–61
"Garden Scape Series No. 17,"
    illustrated, 8–9
Gathorne-Hardy, Jason, painting
    by, 142

Goss, Andrew, et al., structure by, 136
"Gothic Novel," illustrated, 72
"Grace: Homage to Earth and Sky,"
    illustrated, 98–99
"Grandmother," illustrated, 24
"Grape Basket for Growers,"
    illustrated, 146
Greenaway, Victor, bowl by, 12
"Green Fish," illustrated, 84
Greenwood, Ann, fabric by, 86–870

H
Hawksbridge, Joan, art object by,
    40–41
Higby, Sha Sha, sculpture by, 54–55
Hobson, Charles, metronome–mono-
    type by, 150, 164–65
Hogbin, Stephen, et al., structure by,
    136
"House on Wheels," illustrated, 68

I
Illusion:
    and concreteness, 53
    and holography, 55
    of movement, 80
    with sight, 17–20
    and virtual reality, 53–55
    See also Depth.
Images:
    abstract, 119–21
    allegorical, 125
    analytic, 124
    cultural, 76
    fantastic, 121–23
    formalistic, 119
    gestalt of, 119
    iconic, 10, 76, 106
    and language, 6–7
    lyrical, 121–23
    metaphoric, 125
    naturalistic, 117–18
    and place, 141, 145
    self-, and community, 143
    from stories, 145
    symbolic, 124–25
    theft of, 129–31

See also Patterns.
Impressionism, defined, 71
Instrumentalism, as critical stance,
    168–69
Irvine, Steve, vase by, 150, 152

L
"Laird's Landing Letters: Water
    Conservation," illustrated, 105
Lake, Anthony, and Partners, gallery
    by, 38–39
Lewis, Clayton, stamp by, 105
Light:
    chiaroscuro, 37–39
    and Impressionism, 71
    and mood, 62
    quality of, 25–26
    value of, 37, 39
Line:
    directional, 66
    expressive, 62, 63–65
    illusions with, 35–36, 36
    qualities of, 35
    relationships among, 65
    See also Marks
Location:
    and identity, 128
    and time, 134
Louie:
    Jim Hong, ceramic sculpture
        by, 84
    Jim Hong, et al., structure
        by, 136

M
"Magdalene Bridge," illustrated, 126
"Mage," illustrated, 108
Makepeace, John, integrated pro-
    gram of, 140
"Man Ray's Kiss," illustrated, 150,
    164–65
Maps, defined, 76
Marks, evocative, 63
Meaning:
    as content, 168
    and context, 93, 107, 137, 151–54
    and sight, 22
    through materials, 93–94

See also Criticism.
Memory:
    and appearance, 11
    organization of, 147–48
    systems of, 6
"Miss Sailing Arrives for Sunday
    School," illustrated, 104
Miz-Maze Theatre, maze by, 132
Modeling, with computers, 56
Models, defined, 76
Moon, Liz, painting by, 126–27
Motif:
    organization of, 77
    selection of, 76
Movement:
    actual, 80–81
    implied, 79, 80
"Move, The," illustrated, 120
Murry–White, Clive, flag by, 74–75

N

Naturalism, and representation,
    71–73, 118–19
"New Grange II," illustrated, 90
"N Gravity 2," illustrated, 150, 156-57
"Night Sky," illustrated, 74–75

O

Objects:
    discrete, 56
    and meaning, 106
    sensory experience of, 58–59
    and subjects, 107
    transitions in, 56, 57
"Opened by Censor," illustrated,
    112–13
"Orfordness," illustrated, 78
Osthoff, Robert, et al., structure
    by, 136

P

Paper, bowl of, 90
Paradigm, defined, 88
Patterns:
    and chaos, 77–79
    dazzle in, 79–80
    and fractals, 83–85

moire, 35–36
    and motifs, 77–79
    natural, 83–85
    new, 75–76
    organization of, 34, 36
    overused, 81–83
    by proximity, 34
    repeating, 77, 79, 81
    by repetition, 34
    and texture, 85
    transformative, 79
Perception, representing, 62
Perspective:
    aerial, 49
    altering, 51
    and horizon line, 47
    and picture plane, 47, 49–51
    three-point, 49, 52
    two-point, 47–49, 52
    and vanishing points, 47
    See also Illusion.
Photographs, infrared, 8–9
Pilkington, Hugh, building by, 150,
    160–61
"Plate," illustrated, 82
Pointillism, and color, 39, 71
Points:
    contrasting, and pointillism, 39
    focal, 34
    qualities of, 33
Post modernism, and cultural
    identity, 147
Problem solving:
    through purpose, 95–96
    through scientific method,
    96–97
Proportion:
    formula for, 52
    qualities of, 51–52

Q

Quadriforms:
    content of, 23
    development of, x
    as learning aids, 22–23

R

Read, Simon, drawing by, 2
Realism
    See also Naturalism.
Region:
    defined, 139–40
    effects of, 139–40
    forces bearing on, 149
    social ecology of, 140–41
Relationships, dynamic, 65
"Rite of Passage," illustrated, 86
Rosar, Kris, photograph
    by, 8–9

S

Scale, and form, 57
Science, discipline of, 4
Sculpture:
    ceramic, 84
    illustrated, 55, 68
    and mass, 67–69
"Sculpture Moving…in a Thousand…
    Pieces," illustrated, 54
Self, as subject, 102–3
Senses:
    and art experience, 11–13
    and emotional levels, 13
    sight,
        critical, 20–22
        physiology of, 14, 17–21, 21
        psychology of, 21
    touch, 13
Shape:
    and balance, 36–37
    character of, 37
    and space, 36, 37
Shop, defined, 10
Sight:
    and brain, 27
    critical, 20–22
    physiology of, 14, 17–20
    and television, 141–43
    See also Illusion.
Signs, defined, 76, 124
"Silent Boats," illustrated, 100–101
Smutylo, Allen, painting by,
    100–101
Subjects:
    and objects, 107

in various disciplines, 103–6
"Subsurface Dragonfly," illustrated, 40
Sullivan, Emma, photograph by, 32
Symbols, defined, 124–25

T
Television, and imaginative sense, 141–43
Texture:
  for illusion, 65–66
  and pattern, 85
  response to, 67
Thomas, Glynn, etching by, 78
"To Forgotten Fleets," drawing for, 2

"Township," illustrated, 114
Transformation:
  nature of, 88–91
  and separate disciplines, 91

U
"Untitled," illustrated, 64
"Untitled Red and Green," illustrated, 32

V
Value, directional, 66
Vernacular:
  defined, 143
  images from, 145–46

Vessels, scorched ash, 46
Volny, Eva, sculpture by, 60–61

W
Waterer, all-season, illustrated, 94
Waters, Pat, print by, 130
Williams, Anthea, sculpture by, 150, 157
Woollard, John, bowl by, 50

Y
Yoshimoto, Rick, ceramic plate by, 82
Young, William, painting by, 114